ZIONISM

A Basic Reader

Edited by Mordecai S. Chertoff

Herzl Press
New York

CONTENTS

Introduction 1
    Charlotte Jacobson

Zionism Today 3
    Marie Syrkin

"An Obscene Act" 9
    Leonard Garment

A Voice From the Past 10

Weizmann Meets Feisal 11
    Chaim Weizmann

Feisal-Frankfurter Correspondence 12

Sadat Obeys the Koran 14

Zionism and the Arab World 15

Emancipating Africa 21
    Theodor Herzl

Palestine Before Zionism 22

   I. Mark Twain Reports: 1867 22

II. The Empty Land 24
    Ernst Frankenstein

A License to Kill 25

Arab Immigration into Palestine 26
    Moshe Aumann

The Balfour Declaration 30
    Chaim Weizmann

Recognition and Restitution 34
    Abba Hillel Silver

The Jewish Right to Equality 38
    David Ben Gurion

The Growth of Arab Population 40

The Case for a Jewish State 41
    Andrei Gromyko

The Love of Zion 44
    Moshe Sharett

The Enemies of Zionism 46
    Daniel P. Moynihan

Fairness to Arab and Jew 47
    Winston Churchill

King Hussein On Arab-Jewish Cooperation 48

An Adventure in the Human Spirit 49
    Abba Eban

"Our Jewish Pilgrim Fathers" 56
    Louis D. Brandeis

From Israel's Proclamation of Independence 60

Israel in Search of Peace 61
    Golda Meir

What is Zionism? 75
    Yigal Allon

The Jews and Jerusalem 76

The Question of Boundaries 83

The Jerusalem Program 88

MAPS 89

Introduction

The goals of Zionism as a political program and the ideals of Zionism as a social philosophy are no better understood today than they were during the early years of the movement. But while Herzl and his predecessors — and followers — had only ignorance and prejudice to combat, our generation of Zionists must cope with naked hatred.

Both Chaim Weizmann and Moshe Sharett appeared before the *Ad Hoc Committee* on Palestine in October 1947, during hearings on the U.N. Partition Plan for Palestine, and had to respond to Arab charges that Zionism was the new Nazism. Today, Israel's representative at the United Nations meets the charge that "Zionism is a form of racism and racial discrimination."

For years, ever since the birth of the State of Israel, Arab propaganda was centered on the Arab refugees, then on the "rights of the Palestinians," then on the question of boundaries and "occupied Arab lands."

It remained for the Arabs and their allies in the "Social, Humanitarian and Cultural Committee" of the General Assembly to finally come out into the open and declared their abiding — and blinding — hatred for Israel and the movement that produced the Jewish State: Zionism.

We view it as a tribute to Zionism that the votes against it came, by and large, from the right and left-wing dictatorships, while the liberal democracies, which uphold the rights of men, voted against the resolution.

Among those who were "absent", or abstained from voting, and even among those who voted against Zionism, there are those who are genuinely ignorant of what Zionism really is; its philosophy, its attitudes, its very reason for being. Many of the countries they represent were as yet unborn when Israel emerged on the world scene, and their understanding of its history and struggles is warped and distorted by the endless barrage of Arab propaganda within the halls of the U.N.

It remained for Egypt's President Sadat to put the Arab hatred of Israel into perspective by identifying Zionism in terms of such tired old anti-semitic cliches as the one he invoked at the Washington Press Club: Jewish control of Egypt's economy.

The campaign against Zionism continues unabated, and with no respect for truth. To help restore historical truth and make clear the ideological and practical justification for the Zionist Movement and the state it helped create, we present herewith some basic statements by those involved in its history — Arabs, Christians and Jews.

Charlotte Jacobson,
Chairman, World Zionist Organization, American Section
November, 1975

Zionism Today

Marie Syrkin

The cynical drive of the Arab-Communist axis to condemn Zionism as racism so thoroughly obliterates meaning from language that a first reaction is to dismiss the attempt as unworthy of refutation. Surely no literate person aware of recent history or the plain sense of words will take this blather seriously. However, we have been well-schooled in the efficacy of the big lie and have no reason to dismiss Hitler's celebrated propaganda dictum that "something will stick", if a libel is repeated frequently enough. For this reason a brief review of the chief lines of argument is not superfluous. Even though the repetition of ABC's may be tiresome, the orgy of anti-semitic vituperation at the United Nations has made it clear that indifference is a dangerous luxury.

In a striking phrase, Patrick Moynihan, United States ambassador to the United Nations, characterized the "enemies of Zionism" as "the enemies of democracy." This was not hyperbole. By his words Moynihan noted more than the fact that, with few exceptions, the sponsors of the anti-Zionist resolution included the globe's fanatical despotisms, while its opponents were, by and large, the liberal democracies. This division sprang not only from shifting alignments among various power blocs but from an appreciation of the nature of Zionism. For Zionism, uniquely among national liberation movements, has from the outset been impelled by a universalist social vision as integral to its purpose as its national aim. Zionist ideologists from Moses Hess to Herzl, Zionist statesmen like Weizmann or Ben Gurion, were possessed by the conviction that the homeland should be rebuilt "on the basis of social justice." Nor were they modest in their conception as to what social justice meant.

3

A list of the hoary standby's of Zionist rhetoric — "making the desert bloom", "draining the marshes" and "social justice" are embarrassingly familiar. Yet these trite slogans represent not only the aspirations of Zionism but its reality. That Arab enmity deflected Zionism from its ideal course and compelled the Jewish state to expend its energies on thwarting aggression with all the accompanying ills of such a necessity, instead of on the realization of its generous vision is a tragedy of our time.

President Sadat, curiously hailed as a moderate, has reinforced his unabashed support of the anti-Zionist campaign by declaring that Zionism came to the Middle East with "hatred, violence, war, blood." A formidable indictment! A faithful supporter of Hitler in World War II, Sadat still follows the master's technique. What is the record?

To begin with, it is a gross error to assert that Herzl and other early Zionist ideologists callously or stupidly ignored the existence of a native population as Arab propagandists like to charge. On the contrary, Herzl drew an extravagant picture of happy Arab-Jewish coexistence in his Utopian phantasy, *Old-New Land*. Like other Zionist thinkers he naively assumed that the benefits resulting from the transformation of Palestine's arid wastes through Jewish labor and settlement would ensure Arab friendship and cooperation. This conclusion seemed to him so eminently reasonable as to be inevitable. With a romantic's faith in the triumph of good sense and good will he expected no other outcome. Early Zionism continued to share his error.

This confidence was not a patronizing variant of the creed of the white man's burden in the style of 19th century Western imperialism: take over a country rich in natural resources, put the natives to work and they will be grateful for the chance to enjoy the blessings of civilization. The Zionist thesis was based on quite other assumptions. It was predicated not only on the fact that Palestine was the ancient Jewish homeland cherished in memory and prayer, but that it had become waste and barely populated as every report from the Middle East indicated. Most crucial in Zionist consideration was that this wasteland constituted neither a former nor present Arab state, but was a Turkish province under the sway of a remote Sultan who together with absentee Arab landlords exploited the local *fellaheen*.

Before World War I some Arab nationalists welcomed the Jews as possible allies in the struggle for the liberation of "Syria" from the Turks. In this connection it should again be noted that "Palestine" as a separate geographic or historic entity did not then exist in the vocabulary of Arab nationalism. The stretch of land sanctified for Jews as *Eretz Israel* was for Arabs merely "Southern Syria" with no special national character to distinguish it from other Arab territory. Contemporary Palestinian Arab nationalism arose as a late, hostile reaction to the ancient Jewish Palestinian movement. To this day Syrian nationalists envisage a Greater Syria which would swallow up not only Israel but Jordan and Lebanon, and would encompass what they consider an artificially fragmented whole in an unitary Arab state. This lack of a Palestinian Arab presence in Arab nationalism as late as 1948 must be borne in mind if the hopes of Zionist thinkers as well as the rationale of non-Jewish statesmen who advocated a Zionist solution of the Jewish problem are to be understood.

The question of "justice" was central to the Jewish case, presented by Zionists in neo-prophetic terms. British and American statesmen employed the more sober term of "equity." But whether you read Ben Gurion or Weizmann, the statements of Balfour and Churchill, or those of lesser officials entrusted with carrying out the policy of the Balfour Declaration, the reasoning is simple and consistent:

1. The persecuted, homeless Jewish people has longed for restored national independence in Zion for centuries.

2. This Zion is a "tiny notch" — to use Lord Balfour's phrase — in territories liberated by the Allies from the Turks.

3. This "notch" has been fructified and brought to life by the labor of Jewish pioneers. No Arabs are displaced by this process; on the contrary, the Arab population keeps increasing dramatically as the result of the Jewish development of the country.

4. Arab nationalism, which has no fixation on Palestine, is being amply satisfied through the establishment of many independent Arab states. Since the Arabs have received 99% of the liberated land and the Jews less than 1%, this is "equity." The compromise redresses an immense wrong at little substantive cost to any other group.

Admittedly this logic lacks subtlety. It ignores the dynamic of subsequent events with which we are all too familiar. The Arabs, contrary to high-minded expectations, did begrudge the "little notch." Even when the notch was further truncated by the abstraction of Transjordan and later by the Partition Resolution, the ensuing onslaught of the Arab states led to the war and bloodshed to which Sadat refers. But the "war, bloodshed and hatred" were strictly of Arab making, and though they introduced agonizing complications in no way impaired the justice of the Zionist claim.

The moral blocks on which Zionism built its case remain solid no matter what brutal hands seek to topple them. Before the Zionist "return", Palestine was indeed a barely inhabited waste. Read Mark Twain's description of the desolation he saw in 1867. Concluding that Palestine no longer existed save in poetry, the American traveller dismissed the country with an obituary. The Arab population *did* double in the period before Partition, while in the neighboring Arab states the population either remained static or diminished. The Arab standard of living rose with that of the Jews. Read census figures prepared by unenthusiastic British administrators for confirmation. That the peaceful development of Jewish and Arab Palestine was interrupted by the furies fanned by the pro-Nazi Mufti and his cohorts in the Arab world is true. Blame them and his present disciples, not Zionism.

In the thirties, when racist incitement brought fruit in Arab attacks on Jewish farms and kibbutzim, Zionism answered with *havlaga*, "self-restraint", a policy which commanded that attackers should be repelled but that no actions likely to injure the innocent should be initiated. Dissenters within Jewish Palestine and the Zionist movement protested at this "milk-sop" failure to counter terror more forcefully. But the policy held for a time. Inevitably, the aggression to which Israel was subjected by enemies outnumbering her twenty to one, transformed these attitudes. Israel's shift to militancy was dictated not by desire or a changed ideology, but by the desperate struggle to survive.

Arab propagandists, who beguilingly conjure up an image of a flourishing Palestine seized by ruthless Zionist imperialists, know that in the first four decades of this century Zionist pioneers paid extravagantly for every dunam of marsh and desert they restored. And surely even the most gullible are aware that the Jewish state came into being not as the result of force but through solemn international agreements. In 1948, as in later crises, the Jews appealed to their Arab fellow citizens to live with them in equality and friendship. Read the Israeli Declaration of Independence. This hope, too, was destroyed by the preachers of war and hatred. The present occupied territories, as well as the Arab refugee problem, are the direct consequence of Arab invasions successfully repelled by Israel.

Recall Prime Minister Eshkol's last minute plea to the Arab states in June, 1967 to keep the peace. The Arabs, sure of victory, chose war.

Today Israel struggles with the bitter aftermath of the Arab lust for the "extinction" of the Jewish state. Remarkably, even the inescapable pressures of security inherent in this constant, unrelenting effort have not vitally affected the essential character of Zionism. Its egalitarian vision continues to shape the state. Despite the tension of warfare, besieged Israel remains a liberal democracy, alone as such in the Middle East; its Arab citizens enjoy equal rights and six Arabs are members of the Knesset. Even in the wake of sickening outrages government authorities steadfastly protect all Arabs against the wrath of those who seek vengeance for the massacres of their children. The natural rate of increase of Israeli Arabs ranks among the highest in the world. Such is the objective situation that a collection of bloody despotisms and exclusivist Moslem theocracies equate with racism and Apartheid.

A salient feature of Apartheid is the creation of a prosperous society through the exploitation of native labor. The holiest tenet of Zionism in theory and practice has been "self-labor" — an awkward phrase to describe the determination of Jews to rebuild their land through their own physical labor. In their innocence the socialist pioneers assumed that the young lives expended on draining the Emek and watering the Negev would give them an unchallengeable moral claim to the soil they restored, a claim even stronger than their deeds of purchase. Of course, Arab critics were not disarmed: Jews religiously determined to be workers were "discriminating" against Arabs. On the other hand, Arabs who in recent years poured eagerly from the West Bank and Gaza to work for high wages in Israel were being "exploited" by Israeli employers. But none of this carping could change the fact that the green fields and new towns of Israel were the monument to the self-sacrificial toil of Zionist idealists.

Israel has its share of failures and shortcomings of which Israelis themselves are the harshest critics, yet the life and laws of the country provide the clearest refutation to the racist libel. However, one Israeli law comes up regularly for triumphant Arab vilification — the Law of Return. States with rigid, restrictive immigration laws charge that the statute which allows every Jew who so wishes to enter Israel as of right is "racist." The Law of Return was promulgated immediately upon the establishment of Israel to demonstrate to a world that had barred its gates to Jews fleeing from the gas chambers that finally there was one spot on the globe which victims of

anti-semitic persecution could claim as home. Thousands of survivors of the Nazi holocaust and thousands of oriental Jews who
escaped savage discrimination in the Arab countries entered Israel
freely. At last mankind was spared the shameful spectacle of rotting
ships, laden with men, women and children, forbidden entry to
ports which might have saved them from certain death. At the same
time, though Jews were granted automatic citizenship, non-Jews
were not precluded from acquisition of citizenship after a period of
residence in Israel.

The Law of Return was the natural instrument for fulfilling the
purpose of the establishment of Israel — the creation of an independent Jewish state. What point had the Partition Resolution if its
intent could be nullified by the easy device of overwhelming the
small Jewish area by an uncontrolled Arab influx? Israel came into
being to cure the specific affliction of Jewish national homelessness.
No other people was so afflicted. If affirmative action to redress a
long-standing inequity has any meaning, the need to foster Jewish
immigration into Israel is self-evident. Certainly, Arabs boasting oil,
vast territories and twenty-one independent national states are in
no ethical position to dispute Israel's right to be and remain a Jewish
state. Nor can any other national state which cherishes its integrity
nor any other national independence liberation movement which
seeks independence challenge this right.

The course of emergent nationalisms in this century has been
bloody. In Africa, Asia and Europe the world has witnessed massacres, expulsions on a global scale, and the ferocious persecution of
minorities: Uganda, Libya, the Sudan, Biafra, Eritrea, the Soviet
Union, Saudi Arabia, India, Pakistan, Lebanon, the Kurds! This
roster is not a geography lesson but an exercise in memory. Each
name brings to mind mass suffering either inflicted or endured, and
the kind of violence that can accurately be described as racist. It is
therefore ironical but not surprising that the chief perpetrators of
these crimes are the very ones who bay most loudly against Israel
and the Jews.

The resurgent anti-semitism now raging at the United Nations is
the symptom of an old malady. It is racism in its most virulent form.
If not contained, it will destroy the United Nations and once more
infect the globe. It is still not too late for an equitable solution of all
the acerbated problems — including that of the new Arab Palestinian nationalism — which are the legacy of Arab belligerence. Those
who uphold Zionism defend the principles of a rational world order
with equal rights for all peoples, the Jewish people among them.

"An Obscene Act"

Leonard Garment

$\mathbf{M}$y delegation has read the new proposal before us. It is unusually straightforward. It asks to determine "that Zionism is a form of racism and racial discrimination."

As simple as this language is, we are concerned that what may not be fully understood is that this resolution asks us to commit one of the most grievous errors in the 30-year life of this organization.

This committee is preparing itself, with deliberation and foreknowledge, to perform a supreme act of deceit, to make a massive attack on the moral realities of the world.

Under the guise of a program to eliminate racism the United Nations is at the point of officially endorsing anti-semitism, one of the oldest and most virulent forms of racism known to human history. This draft explicitly encourages the racism known as anti-semitism even as it would have us believe that its words will lead to the elimination of racism.

I choose my words carefully when I say that this is an obscene act. The United States protests this act. But protest alone is not enough. In fairness to ourselves we must also issue a warning. This resolution places the work of the United Nations in jeopardy.

The language of this resolution distorts and perverts. It changes words with precise meanings into purveyors of confusion. It destroys the moral force of the concept of racism, making it nothing more than an epithet to be flung arbitrarily at one's adversary. It blinds us to areas of agreement and disagreement, and deprives us of

From statement to U.N. Third Committee, October 17, 1975.

9

the clarity of vision we desperately need to understand and resolve the differences among us. And we are here to overcome our differences, not to deepen them.

Zionism is a movement which has as its contemporary thrust the preservation of the small remnant of the Jewish people that survived the horrors of a racial holocaust. By equating Zionism with racism, this resolution discredits the good faith of our joint efforts to fight actual racism. It discredits these efforts morally and it cripples them politically.

The language of this resolution has already disrupted our efforts here to work together on the elimination of racism and it will continue to do so. Encouraging anti-semitism and group hostility, its adoption would bring to an end our ability to cooperate on eliminating racism and racial discrimination as part of the official work of the Decade.

Once again our failure to reason together has encouraged some delegations to exploit our collective shortcomings and individual vulnerabilities and impede our attempts to further the protection of human rights and fundamental freedoms.

The United Nations, throughout its 30-year history, has not lived by the force of majorities; it has not lived by the force of arms. It has lived only — I repeat, only — because it has been thought that the nations of the world, assembled together, would give voice to the most decent and humane instincts of mankind. From this thought has come the moral authority of the United Nations, and from this thought its influence upon human affairs.

Actions like this do not go unnoticed. They do not succeed without consequences, many of which while only imperfectly perceived at the time soon become an ineradicable part of a new and regrettable reality. Let us make no mistake: at risk today is the moral authority which is the United Nations' only ultimate claim for the support of our peoples.

A Voice From the Past

"The USSR delegation cannot but express surprise at the position adopted by the Arab States on the Palestine question, and particularly at the fact that those States — or some of them, at least — have resorted to such action as sending their troops into Palestine and carrying out military operations aimed at the suppression of the national liberation movement there."

Soviet Ambassador Andrei Gromyko,
UN Security Council, May 21, 1948

Weizmann Meets Feisal

Chaim Weizmann

In the thoughtful declaration which the United States delegates made before this Committee, attention is drawn to the achievement by many Arab peoples of their independence in wide areas. It is appropriate that the question should be viewed in this context of relative equity. The Jews are only claiming in small measure what has been conferred upon the Arabs in abundant degree. There was a time when Arab statesmen were able to see that equity in its true proportions. That was when the eminent leader and liberator of the Arabs, the Emir Feisal, later King of Iraq, made a treaty with me declaring that if the rest of Arab Asia were free, the Arabs would concede the Jewish right freely to settle and develop in Palestine which would exist side by side with the Arab state. My first thought on coming to Palestine in 1918 was to see the Arab leader and to reach such an agreement with him. I shall always be grateful to the British military authority who enabled me to carry out that somewhat hazardous journey into the desert. This agreement was subsequently embodied in the Treaty. The condition which he then stipulated, the independence of all Arab territories outside Palestine, has now been fulfilled. The area of Arab independence stretches from the Euphrates to the Indian Ocean. But independence is not the sole and exclusive right of the Arabs. We Jews also have an equal claim to it. This Assembly cannot possibly decree that the desire of the Arabs to possess an eighth state must obliterate the right of the Jews to possess a single corner where they can live an independent national existence in the land from which they sent a message which became the basis of human civilization.

From testimony before U.N. Special Committee on Palestine, October 18, 1947.

Feisal-Frankfurter
Correspondence

Delegation Hedjazienne, *Paris, March 3, 1919.*

Dear Mr. Frankfurter:

I want to take this opportunity of my first contact with American Zionists to tell you what I have often been able to say to Dr. Weizmann in Arabia and Europe.

We feel that the Arabs and Jews are cousins in race, having suffered similar oppressions at the hands of powers stronger than themselves, and by a happy coincidence have been able to take the first step towards the attainment of their national ideals together.

We Arabs, especially the educated among us, look with the deepest sympathy on the Zionist movement. Our deputation here in Paris is fully acquainted with the proposals submitted yesterday by the Zionist Organization to the Peace Conference, and we regard them as moderate and proper. We will do our best, in so far as we are concerned, to help them through: we will wish the Jews a most hearty welcome home.

With the chiefs of your movement, especially with Dr. Weizmann, we have had and continue to have the closest relations. He has been a great helper of our cause, and I hope the Arabs may soon be in a position to make the Jews some return for their kindness. We are working together for a reformed and revived Near East, and our two movements complete one another. The Jewish movement is national and not imperialist. Our movement is national and not imperialist, and there is room in Syria for us both. Indeed I think that neither can be a real success without the other.

People less informed and less responsible than our leaders and yours, ignoring the need for cooperation of the Arabs and Zionists have been trying to exploit the local difficulties that must necessarily arise in Palestine in the early stages of our movements. Some of them have, I am afraid, misrepresented your aims to the Arab peasantry, and our aims to the Jewish peasantry, with the result that interested parties have been able to make capital out of what they call our differences.

I wish to give you my firm conviction that these differences are not on questions of principle, but on matters of detail such as must inevitably occur in every contact of neighbouring peoples, and as are easily adjusted by mutual goodwill. Indeed nearly all of them will disappear with fuller knowledge.

I look forward, and my people with me look forward, to a future in which we will help you and you will help us, so that the countries in which we are mutually interested may once again take their places in the community of civilised peoples of the world.

Believe me,

Yours sincerely,

(Sgd.) Feisal.
5th March, 1919.

Royal Highness:

Allow me, on behalf of the Zionist Organisation, to acknowledge your recent letter with deep appreciation.

Those of us who come from the United States have already been gratified by the friendly relations and the active cooperation maintained between you and the Zionist leaders, particularly Dr. Weizmann. We knew it could not be otherwise; we knew that the aspirations of the Arab and the Jewish peoples were parallel, that each aspired to reestablish its nationality in its own homeland, each making its own distinctive contribution to civilisation, each seeking its own peaceful mode of life.

The Zionist leaders and the Jewish people for whom they speak have watched with satisfaction the spiritual vigour of the Arab movement. Themselves seeking justice, they are anxious that the just national aims of the Arab people be confirmed and safeguarded by the Peace Conference.

We knew from your acts and your past utterances that the Zionist movement—in other words the national aims of the Jewish people—had your support and the support of the Arab people for whom you speak. These aims are now before the Peace Conference as definite proposals by the Zionist Organisation. We are happy indeed that you consider these proposals "moderate and proper," and that we have in you a staunch supporter for their realisation. For both the Arab and the Jewish peoples there are difficulties ahead—difficulties that challenge the united statesmanship of Arab and Jewish leaders. For it is no easy task to rebuild two great civilisations that have been suffering oppression and misrule for centuries. We each have our difficulties we shall work out as friends, friends who are animated by similar purposes, seeking a free and full development for the two neighbouring peoples. The Arabs and Jews are neighbours in territory; we cannot but live side by side as friends.

Very respectfully,

(Sgd.) Felix Frankfurter

His Royal Highness Prince Feisal.

Sadat Obeys the Koran

The most splendid thing our prophet Muhammad, God's peace and blessing on him, did was to evict them (the Jews) from the entire Arabian peninsula . . . I pledge to you that we will celebrate on the next anniversary God willing, and in this place with God's help, not only the liberation of our land but also the defeat of the Israeli conceit and arrogance so that they may once again return to the condition decreed in our holy book: "Humiliation and abasement has been stamped on them" . . . We will not renounce this.

Egyptian President Anwar el-Sadat
April 25, 1972

Zionism and the Arab World

The Balfour Declaration was part of a general Middle Eastern policy which strove to satisfy and harmonize the aspirations of Jewish and Arab nationalism. There was no atmosphere of incompatibility in those days. Of those concerned with the making of the peace settlement, some, such as Balfour, regarded a Jewish Palestine as a trivial compensation to be demanded of the Arabs in return for the vast independence which they had gained elsewhere. He hoped that "remembering all that, they would not grudge that small notch in what are now Arab territories being given to the people who for all these hundreds of years have been separated from it." Lord Milner considered that the Biblical and international associations of Palestine automatically removed it from the scope of full Arab independence. In the House of Lords, on 27th June, 1923, he said:

"I am a strong supporter of pro-Arab policy. I believe in the independence of the Arab countries. . . . I look forward to an Arab Federation. . . .But Palestine never can be regarded as a country on the same footing as the other Arab countries. You cannot ignore the fact that this is the cradle of all the great religions of the world. It is a sacred land to the Arabs, but it is also a sacred land to the Jew and the Christian; and the future of Palestine cannot possibly be left to be determined by the temporary impressions and feelings of the Arab majority in the country of the present day."

From The Jewish Case, *Anglo-American Committee of Inquiry, Jerusalem, 1946.*

There were others who regarded the concession by the Arabs of Zionist claims not as an act of magnanimity or sacrifice but as one of enlightened self-interest. Sir Mark Sykes, T.E. Lawrence and the Emir Feisal belonged to this category, and Dr. Weizmann lent them fervent encouragement. Feisal appeared at the Peace Conference, directly representing the Arabs of Syria, which then included Palestine, and speaking in the name of his father, who was the sovereign authority in the Arab national movement:

> "In Palestine the enormous majority of the people are Arabs. The Jews are very close to the Arabs in blood, and there is no conflict between the two races. In principles we are absolutely at one. Nevertheless, the Arabs cannot risk assuming the responsibility of holding level the scales in the clash of races and religions that have, in this one province, so often involved the world in difficulties. They would wish for the effective super-position of a great trustee, so long as a representative local administration commended itself by actively promoting the material prosperity of the country."[1]

In the official record of the Peace Conference, the leader of the Arab delegation is quoted as having declared that "Palestine for its universal character he left on one side, for the mutual consideration of all parties interested. *With this exception,* he asked for the independence of the Arabic areas enumerated in the memorandum."[2]

On 3rd January, 1919, the Emir Feisal, representing and acting on behalf of the Arab kingdom of the Hejaz, and Dr. Weizmann, representing and acting on behalf of the Zionist Organisation, signed an agreement in London in the hope of inaugurating a period of good understanding. This agreement spoke of cordial cooperation between the Arab State and Palestine, of the acceptance by the Arabs of the Balfour Declaration and the encouragement of Jewish immigration to Palestine. The Emir added a note of reservation to this effect: "If changes are made, I cannot be answerable for failing to carry out this agreement." This note referred to the establishment of Arab sovereignty in Syria and Iraq as well as in the Arabian Peninsula, where it had already been acknowledged. That changes were made in both countries to the detriment of the Arab interest

---

[1]Palestine Royal Commission Report, 1937, Chapter II, para. 25, p. 26.
[2]"The Truth about the Peace Treaties," David Lloyd George, Vol. II, London, 1938 p. 1042.

was no fault of Dr. Weizmann or of the Jews. The Royal Commission on Palestine, 1936, lucidly summarised the situation thus: "If King Hussein and the Emir Feisal secured their big Arab State, they would concede little Palestine to the Jews." In another comment the Royal Commission points out that the conditions which Feisal hoped would exist in 1922 exist today, now that the independence of all the Arabs outside Palestine has been formally recognised and embodied in the structure of international organisations. And a highly significant passage in the same report reminds the Arabs how little justified they are in grudging the Jews a fraction of what they claim for themselves:

"The fact that the Balfour Declaration was issued in 1917 in order to enlist Jewish support for the Allies and the fact that this support was forthcoming are not sufficiently appreciated in Palestine. The Arabs do not appear to realize in the first place that the present position of the Arab world as a whole is mainly due to the great sacrifices made by the Allied and Associated Powers in the War and, secondly, that, in so far as the Balfour Declaration helped to bring about the Allies' victory, it helped to bring the emancipation of all the Arab countries from Turkish rule. If the Turks and their German allies had won the War, it is improbable that all the Arab countries, except Palestine, would now have become or be about to become independent States."[3]. . .

It is not easy for the Arab world to appear in the guise of an aggrieved or oppressed party. Thirty years ago all Arabs were subject to the ultimate sovereignty of a foreign ruler. Today their area of independence stretches almost without interruption from the Taurus Mountains to the Gulf of Aden and from the Persian Gulf to the Western Mediterranean. Each year sees some new measure enlarging their autonomy and sovereignty in one or the other of these regions. Each year the remnants of Western control become smaller and weaker. In the United Nations and its subsidiary committees the Arabs enjoy a voting power and influence out of all proportion to their essential strength and in excess of that which is enjoyed by many nations with more stable governments and larger cultural assets. The Arabs indeed are the godchildren of modern history, born with a silver spoon in their mouth. Independence has been

---

[3]Palestine Royal Commission Report, 1937, Ch. II, para. 19, p. 24.

lavished upon them — as soon as, or usually before, they could comprehend its full meaning and responsibility. Their liberation was effected primarily by the efforts of Allied armies. Their economic assets were increased and fructified mainly by non-Arab agencies. Whatever the definition of a sated power, the Arabs must surely fulfil it in the highest degree. For, as though this were not enough, they have now emerged from a war which devastated and starved great centres of human habitation without suffering any loss of life or damage to property, enjoying a gross financial advantage from the fact of their strategic and commerical position. It is grotesque to imagine that their position today gives them any right to compete with the Jews on the grounds of need and suffering. Sympathy belongs to those who have suffered: and not merely sympathy, but redress. Against the background of Arab sovereignty, territorial abundance and vast economic opportunity, all obtained at little loss and little sacrifice, we have the sombre picture of the Jewish people, with no voice in international councils, its manpower reduced by a vile and sadistic massacre and its one avenue of potential national opportunity besieged, attacked and almost nagged out of existence by an Arab nationalist movement which could surely find more constructive and liberal things to do. For the idea of a Jewish Palestine threatens neither the existence nor the welfare of the Arab world. It implies no reduction in the main total of the Arabs' political weight. It affects their economic situation only to its advantage. It leaves their specific culture full scope for development in every one of the centres with which it has been historically associated. If the matter is judged purely on the basis of international equity, the Arabs' claim to add Palestine to their large estate is equivalent to the extortion of Naboth's vineyard.

The Arabs at present possess independent monarchies in Saudi Arabia, Yemen, Egypt and Iraq, independent republics in Syria and the Lebanon, and a semi-independent principality in Transjordan, which now also appears to be on the verge of full sovereignty.[4] The area covered by the Arab League is represented by five full members in the Assembly of the United Nations; and one of them, Egypt, is a member of the Security Council. The area and population of

---

[4]Transjordan was originally included in the area governed by the obligation to establish a Jewish National Home. It was detached from the scope of the Balfour Declaration largely in order to satisfy Arab demands.

Palestine's immediate neighbours are as follows:

	Population	Area in sq. km.
Egypt	17,000,000	994,000
Iraq	3,500,000	453,000
Syria	3,000,000	
		181,000
The Lebanon	1,000,000	
Transjordan	300,000	90,000

The area of Palestine is 27,000 square kilometres and its present population less than 1,750,000. The highest figure of Jewish population which has ever entered into the calculations or predictions of responsible statesmen for this generation is 4,000,000 (the figure mentioned by Mr. Winston Churchill on February 8th, 1920). It is far-fetched to assume that Palestine, even at this maximal stage of its development and colonisation, would have the capacity, even if it had the will, to disrupt the general structure of Arab political independence. Very few nations in Europe are endowed with an opportunity equal to theirs — a territory far greater than their population can occupy or cultivate; a powerful voice in international councils; and a strategic position in world communications which makes all the great Powers interested in the stability and progress of their countries. The exclusion of Palestine from the scope of full Arab independence does little to alter the general picture of Arab predominance along the shores of the Eastern Mediterranean and the Indian Ocean. When two parties make a mutually exclusive claim to anything, equity demands that the award should take account of what each already possesses and what each lacks. Justice will be affronted if this criterion is ignored here.

The establishment of political independence in so many Arab countries is often adduced as a compelling reason for extending it to the Palestine Arabs as well. To accept this contention is to decide that a minority status is inadmissible for any Arab community, but right and proper for every Jewish community; that there exists in fact a discrimination between the natural rights of Arabs and Jews whereby the former must be a majority wherever they live and the Jews remain a minority in every country, including that designated by international tribunals as the scene of the National Home. Assuming majority status and political independence to be the essential basis of national existence, it is not difficult to adjudge which of the two peoples possesses it abundantly and which of them lacks it completely. Nor is it the case that the Jews and Arabs would be equally endangered in their elementary rights by being restricted to the status of the minority community in Palestine. For the Arabs, in the contingency of being a minority there, would still be an integral part of a race exercising unchallenged predominance throughout the entire Middle East. They would be surrounded on all sides by kinsmen enjoying the full panoply of sovereign independence and able to intercede on behalf of their Palestine brethren either by their own influence or by invoking international support. Thus their minority status would be formal rather than virtual. It would be impossible for any Jewish authority established in Palestine to show neglect or lack of consideration for the rights of Palestinian Arabs without incurring the immediate and practical displeasure of all their Arab neighbours. The situation would be far different for a Jewish minority crystallised perpetually as such within the borders of an Arab State. For they would have no neighbouring kinsmen whose support could be invoked on their behalf. It they remained a minority community, they could hope for no access to diplomatic or international status such as that which the Arabs enjoy so abundantly. The Palestine Arabs would not feel from the surrounding countries any incentive to encourage liberal treatment of their Jewish minority. The Jews, in fact, in such a situation, would possess no statutory protection of their security other than that which they "enjoyed" in many European countries where they had been established for hundreds of years. In their National Home, as in Eastern and Central Europe, their numbers, opportunities and prospects of development would depend upon the volition of a power external to themselves, with no prior disposition to look favourably upon Jewish progress.

It is sometimes asserted, as in the White Paper of 1939, that the Jewish National Home might find compensation for its minority status by being granted some form of international guarantee. But no judicial rights existing on paper can effectively protect a minority community against measures taken by its own government to restrict or inhibit its liberties. In any case, the system of minority guarantees entirely failed in European States. There is no reason to expect them to succeed in Arab countries, none of which in recent years has evinced a liberal or sympathetic attitude to minority or separatist movements. It is sufficient to recall the experiences of the

Kurds and the Assyrians in Iraq to realise how scanty is the chance of an Arab government's applying the spirit and the principles of federal autonomy in deference to the specific cultural and political characteristics of minority communities. Nor does the depressed status of Jewish communities in Arab countries offer any encouragement. Moreover, Arab leaders in Palestine, though sometimes paying lip-service to the doctrines of egalitarianism, have never concealed their belief that they regard the Jewish National Home as possessing excessive powers and liberties already; and it would obviously be their first care on assuming sovereign independence in Palestine to curtail and restrict the liberties of the Jewish National Home. An Arab political leader, returning recently from internment in Rhodesia, where he had been detained as a person whose liberty would be dangerous to Imperial security, declared that he thought the Jewish population in Palestine should be reduced rather than increased. Another Arab representative suggested to His Excellency the High Commissioner that Jews in Palestine should join their relatives in Europe — presumably in Displaced Persons camps or the ruins of the Warsaw ghetto.[5] A Jewish minority in Palestine could expect neither sympathy nor tolerance from a leadership capable of such crudities. Jews assert that minority status is what they are running away from — not what they go to Palestine for; and they can adduce many proofs in recent history to support the reality of their apprehensions. In short, it is not the case that Arabs and Jews would be making an equal sacrifice or be exposed to equal hazards by accepting a minority position in Palestine.

[5]Quoted in the Arabic journal "Mustaqbal" (January, 1945).

Emancipating Africa

"There is still one problem of racial misfortune unsolved. The depths of that problem, in all their horror, only a Jew can fathom. I mean the negro problem. . . Think of the hair-raising horrors of the slave trade. Human beings, because their skins are black, are stolen, carried off, and sold. Their descendants grow up in alien surroundings despised and hated because their skin is differently pigmented. I am not ashamed to say, though I be thought ridiculous, now that I have lived to see the restoration of the Jews, I should like to pave the way for the restoration of the Negroes."
Theodor Herzl, in "Alt-Neuland", 1902

Palestine Before Zionism

I. Mark Twain Reports: 1867

Of all the lands there are for dismal scenery, I think Palestine must be the prince. The hills are barren, they are dull of color, they are unpicturesque in shape. The valleys are unsightly deserts fringed with a feeble vegetation that has an expression about it of being sorrowful and despondent. The Dead Sea and the Sea of Galilee sleep in the midst of a vast stretch of hill and plain wherein the eye rests upon no pleasant tint, no striking object, no soft picture dreaming in a purple haze or mottled with the shadows of the clouds. Every outline is harsh, every feature is distinct, there is no perspective — distance works no enchantment here. It is a hopeless, dreary, heartbroken land.

Small shreds and patches of it must be very beautiful in the full flush of spring, however, and all the more beautiful by contrast with the far-reaching desolation that surrounds them on every side. I would like much to see the fringes of the Jordan in springtime, and Shechem, Esdraelon, Ajalon, and the borders of Galilee — but even then these spots would seem mere toy gardens set at wide intervals in the waste of a limitless desolation.

Palestine sits in sackcloth and ashes. Over it broods the spell of a curse that has withered its fields and fettered its energies. Where Sodom and Gomorrah reared their domes and towers, that solemn sea now floods the plain, in whose bitter waters no living thing exists — over whose waveless surface the blistering air hangs motionless and dead — about whose borders nothing grows but

From "The Innocents Abroad," 1869

weeds, and scattering tufts of cane, and that treacherous fruit that promises refreshment to parching lips, but turns to ashes at the touch. Nazareth is forlorn; about that ford of Jordan where the hosts of Israel entered the Promised Land with songs of rejoicing, one finds only a squalid camp of fantastic Bedouins of the desert; Jericho the accursed lies a moldering ruin today, even as Joshua's miracle left it more than three thousand years ago; Bethlehem and Bethany, in their poverty and their humiliation, have nothing about them now to remind one that they once knew the high honor of the Saviour's presence; the hallowed spot where the shepherds watched their flocks by night, and where the angels sang, "Peace on earth, good will to men," is untenanted by any living creature and unblessed by any feature that is pleasant to the eye. Renowned Jerusalem itself, the stateliest name in history, has lost all its ancient grandeur and is become a pauper village; the riches of Solomon are no longer there to compel the admiration of visiting Oriental queens; the wonderful temple which was the pride and the glory of Israel is gone, and the Ottoman crescent is lifted above the spot where, on that most memorable day in the annals of the world, they reared the Holy Cross. The noted Sea of Galilee, where Roman fleets once rode at anchor and the disciples of the Saviour sailed in their ships, was long ago deserted by the devotees of war and commerce, and its borders are a silent wilderness; Capernaum is a shapeless ruin; Magdala is the home of beggared Arabs; Bethsaida and Chorazin have vanished from the earth, and the "desert places" round about them, where thousands of men once listened to the Saviour's voice and ate the miraculous bread, sleep in the hush of a solitude that is inhabited only by birds of prey and skulking foxes.

Palestine is desolate and unlovely. And why should it be otherwise? Can the *curse* of the Deity beautify a land?

Palestine is no more of this workday world. It is sacred to poetry and tradition — it is dreamland.

II. The Empty Land

Ernst Frankenstein

At the end of the eighteenth century the land was practically empty. The French traveller Volney, who visited it in 1783-85, characterizes Palestine as one of the most devastated parts of Syria and speaks of the general decay of the country. Gaza, then the capital, had no more than two thousand inhabitants, Jerusalem between twelve and fourteen thousand; Safed, destroyed by an earthquake in 1759, was still an almost deserted village twenty-five years later.

Buckingham, who visited the country in 1816, states that Jaffa "has all the appearances of a poor village, and every part of it that we saw was of corresponding meanness." He visited Ramleh "where, as throughout the greater part of Palestine, the ruined portion seemed more extensive than that which was inhabited." In Rihhah he found the work done by women and children; "the men roam the plains on horseback, and live by robbery and plunder, which form their chief and most gainful occupation."

Thereafter conditions deteriorated further. "In his (Volney's) day," writes Keith in 1843, "the land had not fully reached its last prophetic degree of desolation and depopulation. The population (viz., of the whole of Syria), rated by Volney at two million and a half, is now estimated at half that amount."

This statement corresponds to the observations of other travellers, for instance Olin (1840) who is a specially valuable witness, since he admires the Palestinian ("Syrian") population ("a fine-spirited race

From "Justice for My People," Dial Press, N.Y., 1944

of men") and ridicules the idea of Jewish colonization. According to him "the population is on the decline." In Hebron "many houses are in a dilapidated state and uninhabited"; the once populated region between Hebron and Bethlehem is "now abandoned and desolate" and has "dilapidated towns." In Jerusalem "a large number of houses are in a delapidated and ruinous state"; "the masses really seem to be without any regular employment." In Rihhah "everything at present bears the marks of abject, and, what is unusual in the East, of squalid poverty." In Lydda another observer, Napier, stated that "the greatest poverty, misery, and disease appeared to prevail."

A German Encyclopedia published in 1827 calls Palestine "desolate and roamed through by Arab bands of robbers." Irby, who visited the country in 1817-18, found "not a single boat of any description on the lake (of Tiberias)," an observation made also by Buckingham, who ascribes the fact to "the poverty, and, one must add, the ignorance and the indolence of the people." In 1883 Col. Conder calls Palestine "a ruined land."

The decline of the population was ascribed by Olin to the want of medical knowledge and skill, while the same traveller found abject and squalid poverty, lack of employment, an abandoned and desolate countryside and dilapidated towns. In Syria, the American expedition under Lynch described the desertion of the villages "caused by the frequent forays of the wandering Bedawin," an observation made previously by Volney. Everywhere there was decline and devastation, neglect and oppression by the authorities, ignorance and lack of the most primitive hygienic provisions.

A License to Kill

The UN's anti-Zionist resolutions have been invoked to justify Arab terror. Three days after the UN resolutions were adopted on Nov. 10, 1975 the PLO blew up Jerusalem's Zion Square, killing seven teenagers and wounding dozens more. On Nov. 20, PLO terrorists killed three rabbinical students at a settlement on the Golan Heights.

The Palestine Corner, Radio Damascus, glorified the Jerusalem attacks on Nov. 10: "The Fedayeen take one copy of the resolutions adopted at the UN, mix them with TNT and blow up Zion Square. These resolutions were adopted . . . to enable . . . every inhabitant . . . of the stolen land . . . to carry a copy that will convince him to join the Fedayeen, mix it with dynamite and blow up Zion Square or one of our occupied squares or streets. Now the resolutions . . . are turning into deeds."

Arab Immigration into Palestine

Moshe Aumann

The people of Palestine has lost not only political control over its country but physical occupation of its country as well.
(Fayez A. Sayegh, *Zionist Colonization in Palestine*, Research Centre, Palestine Liberation Organization, Beirut, page V)

. . . land acquired by Jews became extra-territorialized. It ceased to be land from which the Arabs could ever hope to gain any advantage.
(Sami Hadawi, *Palestine in Focus*, Palestine Research Centre, Beirut, 1968, page 29)

Sayegh and Hadawi are two of the most prolific — and vociferous—exponents of the Arab case. In innumerable books, pamphlets and lectures, they and their colleagues and fellow-travellers have repeated this theme of "the Arabs' physical expulsion from Palestine" to the point where it has become the central axiom of Arab propaganda.

That precisely the opposite is true is evident from even the most cursory examination of sources which, by all accounts, must be considered rather more objective and reliable than the two writers we have quoted.

Statistics published in the Palestine Royal Commission Report (p. 279) indicate a remarkable phenomenon: Palestine, traditionally a

---

From "Land Ownership in Palestine: 1880-1948."

country of Arab emigration, became after World War I a country of Arab immigration. In addition to recorded figures for 1920-1936, the Report devotes a special section to illegal Arab immigration. While there are no precise totals on the extent of Arab immigration between the two World Wars, estimates vary between 60,000 and 100,000. The principal cause of the change of direction was Jewish development of the land, which created new and attractive work opportunities and, in general, a standard of living previously unknown in the Middle East.

In one of his major historical works, James Parkes calls the reader's attention to this little-known aspect of the history of Palestine between the two World Wars:

> *The Arab population continued to grow at a phenomenal rate, there was a substantial illegal immigration of Arabs, especially from the Hauran, and Arab prosperity increased through the increased activity of the Jewish community and the many new openings for employment with it offered.*

During World War II, the Arab population influx mounted apace, as is attested by the *UNRWA Review,* Information Paper No. 6 (Sept. 1962):

> *A considerable movement of people is known to have occurred, particularly during the Second World War, years when new opportunities of employment opened up in the towns and on military works in Palestine. These wartime prospects and, generally, the higher rate of industrialization in Palestine attracted many new immigrants from the neighboring countries, and many of them entered Palestine without their presence being officially recorded.*

A major factor in the rapid growth of the Arab population was, of course, the rate of natural increase, among the highest in the world. This was accentuated by the steady reduction of the previously high infant mortality rate as a result of the improved health and sanitary conditions introduced by the Jews and the Mandatory Administration.

Altogether, the non-Jewish element in Palestine's population (not including Bedouin) expanded between 1922 and 1929 alone by more than 75 per cent. The Royal Commission Report makes these interesting observations:

The shortage of land is, we consider, due less to the amount of land acquired by Jews than to the increase in the Arab population. (Page 242)

We are also of the opinon that up till now the Arab cultivator has benefited, on the whole, both from the work of the British administration and from the presence of Jews in the country. Wages have gone up; the standard of living has improved; work on roads and buildings has been plentiful. In the Maritime Plains, some Arabs have adopted improved methods of cultivation. (Page 241)

Jewish development served as an incentive not only to Arab entry into Palestine from Lebanon, Egypt, Syria and other neighbouring countries, but also the Arab population movements within the country — to cities and areas where there were large Jewish concentrations. Some idea of this phenomenon may be gained from the following official figures:

Between the two World Wars, the population count in predominantly Arab towns showed the ordinary natural-increase pattern: in Hebron it rose from 16,650 in 1922 to 22,800 in 1943; Nablus — from 15,931 to 23,300; Jenin — from 2,737 to 3,900; Bethlehem — from 6,658 to 8,800. Gaza's population actually decreased from 17,426 in 1922 to 17,045 in 1931.

On the other hand, in the three major Jewish cities the Arab population shot up, during this period, far beyond the rate of natural increase: Jerusalem — from 28,571 in 1922 to 56,400 (a 97 per cent increase); Jaffa — from 27,437 to 62,600 (134 per cent); Haifa — from 18,404 to 58,200 (216) per cent).

The population of the predominantly Arab Beersheba district dropped, between 1922 and 1939, from 71,000 to 49,000 (the rate of natural increase should have resulted in a rise to 89,000). In the Bethlehem district, the figure increased from 24,613 to about 26,000 (after falling to 23,725 in 1929). In the Hebron area, it went up from 51,345 to 59,000 (the natural increase rate dictated a rise to 72,000).

In contrast to these declines or comparatively slight increases in exclusively Arab-inhabited area, in the Nazareth, Beit Shean, Tiberias and Acre districts — where large-scale Jewish settlement and rural development was under way — the figure rose from 89,600 in 1922 to some 151,000 in 1938 (by about 4.5 per cent per annum, compared with a natural increase rate of 2.5—3 per cent).

In the largely Jewish Haifa area, the number of Arab peasants grew at the rate of 8 per cent a year during the same period. In the heavily Jewish-populated Jaffa and Ramla districts, the Arab rural population grew from 42,300 to some 126,000 — an annual increase of 12 per cent, or more than four times as much as can be attributed to natural increase.

One reason for the Arab gravitation towards Jewish-inhabited area, and from neighbouring countries to Palestine, was the incomparably higher wage scales paid there. . .

There is perhaps no better way to conclude and sum up this study than to cite two very different sources, both of which have figured in our documentation — the Peel Commission Report and Abdel Razak Kader. The two quotations we have chosen have this in common that both underline the same basic truth in this fateful chapter of Jewish-Arab relations that has been so heavily beclouded by willful distortion and possibly, by an overactive imagination.

First — the Peel Commission Report (p. 242):

The Arab charge that the Jews have obtained too large a proportion of good land cannot be maintained. Much of the land now carrying orange groves was sand dunes or swamp and uncultivated when it was purchased . . . there was, at the time at least of the earlier sales, little evidence that the owners possessed either the resources or the training needed to develop the land.

The second quotation is from the article cited earlier, by the Algerian-in-exile Kader, who, proceeding to reply to his own query, "Is Israel a thorn or a flower in the Near East?", writes:

The nationalists of the states neighbouring on Israel, whether they are in the government or in business, whether Palestinian, Syrian or Lebanese, or town dwellers of tribal origin, all know that at the beginning of the century and during the British Mandate the marshy plains and stony hills were sold to the Zionists by their fathers or uncles for gold — the very gold which is often the origin of their own political or commerical careers. The nomadic or semi-nomadic peasants who inhabited the frontier regions know full well what the green plains, the afforested hills and the flowering fields of today's Israel were like before.
The Palestinians who are today refugees in the neighbouring countries and who were adults at the time of their flight know all this, and no anti-Zionist propaganda — pan-Arab or pan-Moslem — can make them forget that their present nationalist exploiters are the worthy sons of their feudal exploiters of yesterday, and that the thorns of their life are of Arab, not Jewish, origin.

The Balfour Declaration

Chaim Weizmann

What did the Balfour Declaration mean? It meant something quite simple at that time, and I am saying so advisedly. It meant that Judaea was restored to the Jews or the Jews were restored to Judaea. I could submit to the Commission a series of utterances of responsible statesmen and men in every walk of life in England to show that this Declaration was at the time regarded as the *Magna Charta* of the Jewish people; it was in a sense comparable with another Declaration made thousands of years before, when Cyrus allowed a remnant of the Jews to return from Babylon and to rebuild the Temple. To the ordinary man at that time reading the Declaration, what it meant is broadly indicated by the various speeches at a solemn meeting at the Opera House in London, where (among others) Lord Cecil spoke and said:—"Arabia for the Arabs, Judaea for the Jews, Armenia for the Armenians." Much water and much blood have flowed under the various bridges of the world since that time, and not all of his predictions have been realized; but we read into the Declaration what the statesmen of Great Britain told us it meant. It meant a National Home, "National" meaning that we should be able to live like a nation in Palestine, and "Home" a place where we might live as free men in contradistinction to living on sufferance everywhere else. To English people I need not explain what the

An excerpt from the statement made before the Palestine Royal Commission in Jerusalem on November 25, 1936.

word "home" means, or what it does *not* mean, to us everywhere else.

The meaning was clear, and the Jewry of the world, in the trenches of Europe, in the pogrom-swept area of Russia, saw it like that. Tens of thousands of Jews marched before the house of the British Consul in Odessa at the time. Behind them were half-organized bands of marauders and murderers sweeping the countryside and destroying everything in their wake. But those Jews poured out their hearts in gratitude to the one accessible representative of the British Government, whom they had never seen, of whom they had never heard, whose language they could not speak, whose mentality they could not understand. They felt that here something had been done for us which, after two thousand years of hope and yearning, would at last give us a resting-place in this terrible world. I can only refer the Commission to the numerous newspaper articles in the British and American press. On the other hand the German Government, when they got to know of it afterwards, were sick at heart that the British had stolen a march on them. They called together our representatives in Germany and tried to explain to them that of course they would have done it, but they could not do it, because they were linked up with Turkey and had to go slowly. Perhaps the German Government considered it a piece of propaganda, but neither the British Government nor the Jews ever conceived of it as such. There was nobody to win over. As I have said, the rich Jews, who could have helped with their influence or money,—to them it meant nothing. The poor Jews had nothing to give.

It meant, as I say, at that time, and speaking in political parlance, a Jewish State; and when I was asked at the Peace Conference, quite impromptu, by Mr. Lansing, "What do you mean by a Jewish National Home?" I gave this answer: "To build up something in Palestine which will be as Jewish as England is English." Of course, we have always borne in mind, and our teachers and mentors at that time, British statesmen, repeatedly told us: "There is a second half to the Balfour Declaration. That second part provides that nothing should be done which might injure the interests of the non-Jewish communities in Palestine." Well, I must leave it to the Commission to test this and to ascertain whether, throughout the work of these last sixteen years, we have done anything which has in any way

injured the position of the non-Jewish population. I go further than
that. The Balfour Declaration says that the civil and religious rights
of the non-Jewish communities should not be interfered with. I
would humbly ask the Commission to give the broadest possible
interpretation to that, not merely a narrow interpretation of civil and
religious rights; put it as broadly as the Commission may wish, and
test it, and I think I can say before the Commission, before God, and
before the world, that in intention, consciously, nothing has been
done to injure their position. On the contrary, indirectly we have
conferred benefits on the population of this country. I should like to
be perfectly frank: We have not come for that purpose. We have
come for the purpose of building up a National Home for the Jewish
people; but we are happy and proud that this upbuilding has been
accompanied by considerable benefits to the country at large.

A certain time elapsed, My Lord, between the issue of the Declaration and the reign of peace in the world—a precarious
peace—before we were allowed, under the terms of the Declaration,
to begin our work; and I should like briefly to describe to the Commission what were the conditions under which we had to begin this
kind of work. I think it will be admitted, after the Royal Commission
has had an opportunity of surveying what we have done, that for
the first time in the history of colonization work of this kind has
been carried out by a private body, a body which had no treasury at
its back, no State organization to aid it, so that we began our work,
so to speak, with our right hand tied. Russian Jewry, that Jewry
which was the natural carrier of the Zionist ideal and Zionist tradition, was broken, non-existent to all intents and purposes. As I have
already mentioned, the rich Jews in the Western communities were,
with a few exceptions, either skeptical or opposed. One of the exceptions, whose work you will no doubt have plenty of opportunity
of seeing, was Baron Edmond de Rothschild, who began his work in
Palestine when it was still under the rule of the Turk. He began his
work here roughly sixty years ago. With perhaps the exception of
him and a few others—very few—the powerful Jews were either
indifferent or against us. In order to get funds for immigration,
settlement, acquisition of land, we had to go hat in hand to the Jews
of the world, to the poor, and get their contributions.

It is, if I may say so with respect, a fallacy to think that what has
been built up in Palestine (with the exception which I have mentioned) has been built up by the rich Jews. When people speak of

Jews, My Lord, they often have in mind the sort of conventional, not to say vulgar, picture of the Jew—powerful, greedy, rapacious, grasping. Here he is, he will throw himself upon a country like a vulture, and will tear it to bits. I have no such opinion even of the rich Jews (I think they are much better than they are made out to be), and certainly not of the poor.

I was instrumental in raising a great part of the public funds which have been sunk in this country. Between 1920 and the present day I have been in America eleven times, once in South Africa, innumerable times in various parts of Europe, and I know my clientèle, so to speak. They are the poor and the lower middle-class; and when I speak of the poor Jew, he is very poor. Only since 1929, since the formation of the extended Jewish Agency, has Palestine become a sort of practical proposition—when people think of practical things nowadays, they do not reckon with imponderables, and do not understand that money is much less than the ideal, the impulse, the self-sacrifice of thousands and thousands who are ready to go to Palestine at the first opportunity—it became a sort of practical proposition, and we began to get the support of the so-called practical men; but at the beginning we had to work in a small country, impoverished, ruined after the War, ruined after four hundred years of misrule by the Turk. Very often British officials used to look at me, and you could feel they were thinking: Dr. Weizmann is not a bad fellow, but he is running his head against a brick wall; what can he make out of this impoverished, difficult country? In 1930, Lord Passfield, a very practical man, a great economist, said to me, "But Dr. Weizmann, do you not realize there is not room enough to swing a cat in Palestine?" I do not want to be facetious, but many a cat has been swung in Palestine since then, and the population of the country has increased, since that talk of mine with Lord Passfield, by something like 200,000.

Those were the conditions under which we had to start: no treasury, no funds, no experience, no training, a broken-up people; a people which for centuries had been divorced from agricultural pursuits, from what is called, in the English language, pioneering. They were petty traders, middlemen, intellectuals—but we began. After fifteen years we stand before an achievement on which I think one can look with a certain amount of respect, and on which, I will not hide from you, we look with a certain amount of pride. . . .

Recognition and Restitution

Abba Hillel Silver

The movement to reconstitute the Jewish commonwealth in Palestine is not a recent movement. It did not begin with modern Zionism, nor with the first Zionist colonies which were established in Palestine 65 years ago. The ideal of national restoration dates from the year of the destruction of Jerusalem and of the Temple in the year A.D. 70, and from the beginning of the widespread dispersion of the Jewish people.

Throughout the following centuries the hope of rebuilding their national home was never absent from among our people. Modern Zionism is only the latest expression of that undeviating will to national restoration which has persisted throughout the ages.

For fifteen centuries and more prior to the time of the great Dispersion, the Jewish people lived in Palestine as a nation, undergoing all the changing political vicissitudes which all nations, large or small, are bound to experience over a long period of time.

During some of those centuries they made their greatest contribution to civilization in the religious field. They gave the Bible to the world and formulated the great spiritual and ethical ideals of mankind. In Palestine and from the Jewish Nation came both Judaism and Christianity.

Whenever disaster threatened their national existence, they found strength to surmount it. The destruction of the first temple in the sixth century B. C., and the exile of the best part of Israel to Babylonia did not result in the death of the nation. By the rivers of Babylon they sat down and wept as they remembered Zion, and in their exile they vowed: "If I forget thee, O Jerusalem, may my right hand forget her cunning."

From testimony before the House Committee on Foreign Affairs, February, 1944.

In the second pre-Christian century, the Jews revolted against their Syrian overlords and regained their political independence. A century later they lost it again to the Romans. When the oppression of the Romans became too great, they revolted again. This great revolt lasted for 6 years, until 70 A. D., when Jerusalem and the temple were destroyed. But the Jewish Nation did not perish then. In 115 the Jewish people revolted again. And in 135 they revolted a third time. Determinedly they resisted the greatest empire of the earth in defense of their national life and liberties.

In the following centuries and as a result of persecution, Jewish life in Palestine sharply declined from its high levels, but it continued in a relatively large scale up to the seventh century, when we again hear of Jews fighting for their freedom. Jews clung to Palestine all through Roman, Byzantine, Arab, Christian, and Turkish domination, to this very day. "Throughout the ages, even in the darkest periods of the Crusades, the protracted wars of the Middle Ages, and in modern times, the Jews never entirely left the soil of Palestine." They never surrendered the hope that some day they would rebuild their national life there. The bitter experiences of 2,000 years of exile, outlawry, ghettos, and massacres only served to reinforce that hope.

The effort to return to Palestine was unremitting through the ages. The living bond with Palestine was never broken. The hope of return became part of the Jews' creed. It echoed through the pages of his prayer book. His festivals were redolent of memories and hopes of Palestine. The Messianic hope which sustained the spirits of our people throughout the bleak centuries was essentially the hope of Israel's return to the Palestine. All through the Middle Ages, when traveling was most difficult and dangerous, Jews found ways singly or in groups, to return to Palestine.

In the nineteenth century this age-old national aspiration finally entered the phase of political organization and practical action.

Orthodox rabbis and lay leaders, moved by convictions both religious and national, were among the first to advocate planned and concerted colonization projects to Palestine.

A strong urge towards political action for national emancipation came also from the circles of Jews of western Europe who had become disillusioned with the results of the nineteenth century enlightenment and emancipation. Sudden and violent outbursts of anti-Semitism in unexpected places forced upon these Jews who had so sanguinely awaited the early liquidation of the Jewish problems, the necessity of taking stock of their position anew.

They realized that the problem of the national homelessness of the Jewish people was the principal source of the Jewish millennial tragedy and that it remained as stark and as menacing as ever. It simply could not be circumvented by wishful thinking or pleasant daydreaming.

These Jews began to look for the basic solution of the problem and they soon discovered it. Fundamentally the root of all the trouble was that the Jewish people was a national homeless people in the world and the only solution for national homelessness is a national home.

Great thinkers from among the intellectual circles of westernized Europe Jewry formulated this new insight and conviction. The theme common to all was emancipation through national restoration. Not that all Jews should return to Palestine any more than that all Englishmen in all parts of the world should return to England, or all Frenchmen to France, or all Germans to Germany. Every nation today has many of its former nationals, citizens of other countries. The Jews in other parts of the world will remain as heretofore loyal citizens of the country which will permit them to remain equal citizens of those countries, and the American Jews, who have served their country so faithfully both in peace and in war, intend to remain citizens of the United States, and their relationship with the Jewish commonwealth will be no different from that of other American citizens with respect to their ancestral homes. But, just as there is an England, a France, and a Germany, so must there be a Land of Israel in order that the status of the Jewish people might be normalized throughout the world. Politically the Jewish people as a people must become, like every other people, possessed of an independent life in a national home.

In 1897, Theodore Herzl convoked the first Zionist Congress at Basle, Switzerland. There the official Zionist platform was adopted: "The aim of Zionism is to create for the Jewish people a home in Palestine secured by public law."

Within 20 years of the organization of modern political Zionism, the movement received formal approval at the hands of the greatest empire on earth — Great Britain.

On November 2, 1917, Arthur James Balfour, then Secretary of State for Foreign Affairs, issued the famous declaration in the name of the British Government.

His Majesty's Government views with favor the establishment in Palestine of a national home —

note the term "national" —

for the Jewish people, and will use their best endeavors to facilitate the achievement of this object, it being clearly understood that nothing shall be done which may prejudice the civil and religious rights of existing non-Jewish communities in Palestine, or the rights and political status enjoyed by Jews in any other country.

The Balfour Declaration, which represents a turning point in the history of the Jewish people, was not, as has sometimes been represented, a purely British formulation of policy. It was for many months the subject of long and earnest negotiation between the principal Allied Powers. In February and March of 1918 the French and Italian Governments, respectively, issued parallel statements in support of the Balfour Declaration. President Wilson had followed the negotiations, and had encouraged the issuance of that declaration, and our Government insisted on having a hand in the drafting of the mandate.

At a meeting of the Supreme Council of the Allied Powers, held at San Remo in April 1920, the Balfour Declaration was unanimously adopted and embodied in the Mandate for Palestine which was offered to Great Britain.

On July 24, 1922, the Council of the League of Nations unanimously ratified the British mandate, with the incorporated declaration as an integral part. That same year the Congress of the United States adopted the resolution which has been read to you this morning:

Resolved by the Senate and House of Representatives of the United States of America in Congress assembled, That the United States of America favors the establishment in Palestine of a national home for the Jewish people, it being clearly understood that nothing shall be done, etc. —

And then occurs the rest of the Balfour Declaration.

The preamble to the mandate contains this significant clause, and I would like to call it to your attention:

Whereas recognition has hereby been given to the historical connections of the Jewish people with Palestine and the grounds for reconstituting their national home in that country * * *

These are the words of the preamble of the mandate. In other words, the creation, or reconstitution, of a Jewish homeland in Palestine was thus accepted as a world policy. It was also regarded as an act of restitution. It was a recognition both of the present need of the Jewish people and of the continuity of its claim to its homeland, a continuity unbroken by the vicissitudes of 2,000 years of history.

The Jewish Right to Equality

David Ben Gurion

Our case it seems to us is simple and compelling, and it rests on two elementary principles: one, that we Jews are just like other human beings, entitled to the same rights as every human being in the world, and we Jewish people are just like any other people, entitled to the same equality of treatment as any free and independent people in the world. The second principle is: this always has been, and will remain our country. We are here as of right. We are not here on the strength of the Balfour Declaration or the Palestine Mandate. We were here long, long before. I myself was here before. Many thousands were here before me, and our people were here for centuries and millennia before that. It is the Mandatory power that is here—legally speaking—on the strength of the Mandate. Our case, and I think you have just seen many such cases in Europe, is like that of the Jews who were forcibly expelled from their homes, which were then given to somebody else. Those homes changed hands, and then after the Nazi defeat some Jewish owners came back and found their houses occupied. In many cases they were not allowed to return to their houses. To make it more exact, I shall put it this way. It is a large building, the building of our family, say 50 rooms. We were expelled from that house, our family was scattered, somebody else took it away and again it changed hands many times, and then we had to come back and we found some five rooms occupied by other people, the other rooms destroyed and uninhabitable from neglect. We said to these occupants, "We do not

From testimony before the Anglo-American Committee of Inquiry, March, 1946.

want to remove you, please stay where you are, we are going back into the uninhabitable rooms, we will repair them." And we did repair some of them and settled there. . . .

One reason for our return is love of Zion, a deep passionate love, strong as death, the love of Zion. There is no parallel to that in all human history. It is unique, but it is a fact; you will see it here. There are 600,000 of us here because of that deep, undying love of Zion.

In evidence given to you in America, an American Arab, I believe it was John Hassan, said there was never a Palestine as a political and geographical entity; and another American Arab, a great Arab historian, Dr. Hitti, went even further and said, and I am quoting him, "There is no such thing as Palestine in history, absolutely not." And I agree with him. (That is not the only thing on which I agree with Arabs.) I agree with him entirely; there is no such thing in history as Palestine, absolutely, but when Dr. Hitti speaks of history he means Arab history, he is a specialist in Arab history and he knows his business. In Arab history there is no such thing as Palestine. Arab history was made in Arabia, in Persia and in Spain and North Africa. You will not find Palestine in that history, nor was Arab history made in Palestine. There is not, however, only Arab history; there is world history and Jewish history and in that history there is a country by the name of Judaea, or as we call it, Eretz Israel, the Land of Israel. We have called it Israel since the days of Joshua the son of Nun. There was such a country in history, there was and it is still there. It is a little country, a very little country, but that little country made a very deep impression on world history and on our history. This country made us a people; our people made this country. No other people in the world made this country; this country made no other people in the world. Now again we are beginning to make this country and again this country is beginning to make us. It is unique, but it is a fact. This country came into world history through many wars, fought for its sake by Egyptians, Babylonians, Assyrians, Persians, Greeks, Romans, Byzantines and others, but it was not these wars that gained it its place. It gained its own place in history. Our country won its place in world history as not many other countries have done, even bigger and richer countries, for one reason only: because our people created here, perhaps a limited, but a very great civilisation, which became the heritage of the whole of humanity. This country shaped our people, the Jewish people, to make it what it has been from then until today: a very exclusive people on one side and a universal people on the other; very national and very international. Exclusive in its internal life and its attachment to its history, to its national and religious tradition; very universal in its religious, social and ethical ideas. We were told that there is one God in the entire world, that there is unity of the human race because every human being was created in the image of God, that there ought to be and will be universal brotherhood and social justice, peace between peoples. Those were our ideas, this was our culture; and this was what won this country its place in world history. We created here a book, many books; many were lost, many remained only in translations, but a considerable number, some twenty-four, remain in their original language, Hebrew, in the same language, Mr. Chairman, in which I am thinking now when I am talking to you in English, and which the Jews in this country are speaking now. We went into exile, we took that book with us and in that book, which was more to us than a book—it was ourselves, we took with us our country in our hearts, in our soul. There is such a thing as a soul, as well as a body, and these three—the land, the book and the people—are one for us forever. It is an indissoluble bond. There is no material power which can dissolve it except by destroying us physically. . . .

The Growth of Arab Population

"*** The Arabs cannot say that the Jews are driving them out of their country. If not a single Jew had come to Palestine after 1918, I believe the Arab population of Palestine would still have been 'round about the figure 600,000 at which it had been stable under Turkish rule. It is because the Jews who have come to Palestine bring modern health services and other advantages that Arab men and women who would have been dead are alive today, that Arab children who would never have drawn breath have been born and grown strong. It is not only the Jews who have benefited from the Balfour Declaration. They can deny it as much as they like, but materially the Arabs in Palestine have gained very greatly from the Balfour Declaration."

Statement by Mr. Malcolm MacDonald, British Secretary of State for the Colonies (Parliamentary Debates, House of Commons, November 24, 1938).

The Case for a Jewish State

Andrei Gromyko

As is well known, the aspirations of an important part of the Jewish people are bound up with the question of Palestine, and with the future structure of that country. It is not surprising, therefore, that both in the General Assembly and in the meetings of the Political Committee of the Assembly a great deal of attention was given to this aspect of the matter. This interest is comprehensible and completely justified. The Jewish people suffered extreme misery and deprivation during the last war. It can be said, without exaggeration, that the sufferings and miseries of the Jewish people are beyond description. It would be difficult to express by mere dry figures the losses and sacrifices of the Jewish people at the hands of the Fascist occupiers. In the territories where the Hitlerites were in control, the Jews suffered almost complete extinction. The total number of the Jews who fell at the hands of the Fascist hangmen is something in the neighborhood of six million. Only about one and a half million Jews survived the war in Western Europe. But these figures, which give an idea of the losses suffered by the Jewish people at the hands of the Fascist aggressors, give no idea of the situation in which the great mass of the Jewish people find themselves after the war.

A great many of the Jews who survived the war in Europe have found themselves deprived of their countries, of their shelter, and of means of earning their livelihood. Hundreds of thousands of Jews are wandering about the various countries of Europe, seeking

From a Speech by Andrei Gromyko, Soviet Delegate to the UN, at the UN General Assembly, May 14, 1947.

a means of livelihood and seeking shelter. A great many of these are in the camps for displaced persons, where they are continuing to suffer great privations.

The experience of the past, particularly during the time of the Second World War, has shown that not one state of Western Europe has been in a position to give proper help to the Jewish people and to defend its interests, or even its existence, against the violence that was directed against it from the Hitlerites and their allies. This is a very serious fact, but unfortunately, like all facts, it must be recognized. The fact that not a single Western European state has been in a position to guarantee the defense of the elementary rights of the Jewish people or compensate them for the violence they have suffered at the hands of the Fascist hangmen explains the aspiration of the Jews for the creation of a state of their own. It would be unjust not to take this into account and to deny the right of the Jewish people to the realization of such an aspiration . . .

In analyzing the various types of plans for the future of Palestine, it is necessary first of all to take into account the specific aspect of this question. We must bear in mind the incontestable fact that the population of Palestine consists of two peoples, Arabs and Jews. Each of these has its historical roots in Palestine. That country has become the native land of both these peoples, and both of them occupy an important place in the country economically and culturally. Neither history nor the conditions which have arisen in Palestine now can justify any unilateral solution of the Palestine problem, either in favor of the creation of an independent Arab state, ignoring the lawful rights of the Jewish people, or in favor of the creation of an independent Jewish state, ignoring the lawful rights of the Arab population. Neither of these extreme solutions would bring about a just settlement of this complex problem, first and foremost since they both fail to guarantee the regulation of the relations between Arabs and Jews, which is the most important task of all. A just settlement can be found only if account is taken in sufficient degree of the lawful interests of both peoples . . .

●

The opponents of the partition of Palestine into two separate, independent, democratic States usually point to the fact that this decision would, as they allege, be directed against the Arabs, against the Arab population in Palestine and against the Arab States in general. This point of view is, for reasons that will be readily understood, particularly emphasized by the delegations of the Arab countries. But the USSR delegation cannot concur in this view. Neither the proposal to partition Palestine into two separate, independent States nor the decision of the *Ad Hoc* Committee that was created at that session and which approved the proposal which is now under discussion, is directed against the Arabs. This decision is not directed against either of the two national groups that inhabit Palestine. On the contrary, the USSR delegation holds that this decision corresponds to the fundamental national interests of both peoples, that is to say, to the interests of the Arabs as well as of the Jews.

The representatives of the Arab States claim that the partition of Palestine would be an historic injustice. But this view of the case is unacceptable, if only because, after all, the Jewish people has been closely linked with Palestine for a considerable period in history. Apart from that, we must not overlook—and the USSR delegation drew attention to this circumstance originally at the special session of the General Assembly—we must not overlook the position in which the Jewish people found themselves as a result of the recent world war. I shall not repeat what the USSR delegation said on this point at the special session of the General Assembly. However, it may not be amiss to remind my listeners again that, as a result of the war which was unleashed by Hitlerite Germany, the Jews, as a people, have suffered more than any other people. You know that there was not a single country in Western Europe which succeeded in adequately protecting the interests of the Jewish people against the arbitrary acts and violence of the Hitlerites . . .

The solution of the Palestine problem based on a partition of Palestine into two separate states will be of profound historical significance, because this decision will meet the legitimate demands of the Jewish people, hundreds of thousands of whom, as you know, are still without a country, without homes, having found temporary shelter only in special camps in some western European countries. I shall not speak of the conditions in which these people are living; these conditions are well known. Quite a lot has been said on this subject by representatives who share the USSR delegation's point of view in this matter, and which support the plan for partitioning Palestine into two States.

From U.N. Speech of Nov. 26, 1947.

The Love of Zion

Moshe Sharett

Invoking the right of possession, the delegate for Pakistan and others argued that Palestine was not Great Britain's property for her to promise it to the Jews. But, for that matter, nor were Syria or Iraq Great Britain's, and yet her promises in their regard were accepted as binding pledges. The Arabs, it was argued, had fought on the side of the Allies in World War I. But so did the Jews, their volunteer legions having come to Palestine from England, United States, Canada, Argentine, and from Palestine itself, to take part in the country's liberation. It is an established fact that Palestine Arabs had no share whatsoever in the fighting. In the final analysis it was the exertions, sacrifices and final victory of Allied armies which resulted in the liberation of Palestine and the Arab provinces. It is to that victory that most independent Arab States of today owe their existence. If they accept the boon of independence which fell into their lap like a ripe plum, they must accept its price. The pledge to grant the Arabs independence in large areas and the setting aside of Palestine for the Jewish people were organic parts of the same war settlement . . .

The Jewish people was born in Palestine and shaped by it. The country gave birth to no other people either before or after. It is untrue that the Jews all left Palestine in the first century. Their mass settlement in Palestine persisted till the seventh century despite persecutions, expulsions and the ruthless crushing of rebellions. Nor is it true that the Jews have ever turned their backs on Palestine.

From testimony before U.N. Palestine Committee, October 18, 1947.

44

Their efforts to return have never ceased and the present phase of resettlement which began in the late seventies of the last century is but the last link in the chain. Zionism did not start with the Balfour Declaration. The Declaration was the product, not the origin of Zionism. The Jewish State idea is not a crazy whim of recent origin. It is the dream of centuries of Jewish martyrdom, the vision of Jews in all generations, the practical ideal which animated the first returning pioneers of seventy years ago. Both the anomalous position of the Jewish people in the diaspora and the remedy urged by Zionism for it are products of history and the whole problem cannot be understood outside its context . . .

I might here recall one curious slur passed on our work by the representative of Egypt who said that all we do in Palestine is artificial. I wonder exactly what he meant by that term and how it was intended to impress us. Go and tell our children who were born in the country that they are artificial. Tell that to the trees we have planted, to the fields we have reclaimed, to the factories in which we are working. Try and dismiss as artificial the potash plant on the Dead Sea or the power house on the Jordan. In this sense the Dam of Assuan in Egypt is artificial. So is the Tennessee Valley project. So is, in fact, the entire magnificent civilization of this American continent, which is all the result of migration . . .

The tone and even the language of most of the speeches of the Arab delegates make it difficult for me to address a word of appeal to them. But let us all think of the common people in Palestine, Arabs and Jews. Let us think of the common people throughout the Middle East. Let us think of those who meet each other in the fields, who rub shoulders on the railways, who do business together or at least would have liked to do business together. They are all, fundamentally, interested in the same things. They all want bread and work, better living conditions, decent homes, good roads, schools for their children, more efficient communications. Naturally, they all want to see their national cultures flourish, and their peoples secure and independent, sharing in the dignity and happiness which free life and enlightened citizenship can offer. There is strife today. There is fear and there is hatred. But beneath it all, there is an upsurging of common human feeling which is bound to assert itself. The returning Jew passionately believes that he belongs to that country, to that part of the world. He is a returning native. He knows there is room for him there. He has proved it. He does not take room away. He gives. He has a great deal to learn. He has something to teach. He wants equality, nothing more, nothing less — the same opportunity, the same status. His neighbors all have their states. He must have his own Jewish State. Nothing in the world will eradicate from his heart the love of Zion. Nothing will stifle in his soul the urge for freedom in his own land. If he is robbed of his due he will not submit. But he wants peace. He knows that one day he will be understood and accepted as an equal. He prays that day may be near.

"THE ENEMIES OF ZIONISM ARE THE ENEMIES OF DEMOCRACY."

✱

The United Nations has become a locus of a general assault by the majority of the nations in the world on the principles of liberal democracy which are now found only in a minority of nations, and for that matter a dwindling minority. It was not Zionism that was condemned at the United Nations on Friday, it was Israel; and not the State of Israel nearly so much as the significance of Israel as one of the very few places, outside of Western Europe and North America and a few offshore islands, where western democratic principles survive, and of all such places, currently the most exposed . . .

This reckless act was adopted by 70 votes to 29, with 27 abstentions . . . A wholesale decision of the despotisms of the right in the world to side with the despotisms of the left, in common concert against the liberal democracies of the center. It was an awful occasion, but it had about it, most of all, the awfulness of truth.

Daniel P. Moynihan,
U.S. Ambassador to the U.N.

Fairness to Arab and Jew

Winston Churchill

To whom was the pledge of the Balfour Declaration made? It was not made to the Jews of Palestine, it was not made to those who were actually living in Palestine. It was made to world Jewry and in particular to the Zionist associations. It was in consequence of and on the basis of this pledge that we received important help in the War, and that after the War we received from the Allied and Associated Powers the Mandate for Palestine. This pledge of a home of refuge, of an asylum, was not made to the Jews in Palestine but to the Jews outside Palestine, to that vast, unhappy mass of scattered, persecuted, wandering Jews whose intense, unchanging, unconquerable desire has been for a National Home. . .

I cannot feel that we have accorded to the Arab race unfair treatment after the support which they gave us in the late War. The Palestinian Arabs, of course, were for the most part fighting against us, but elsewhere over vast regions inhabited by the Arabs independent Arab kingdoms and principalities have come into being such as had never been known in Arab history before. Some have been established by Great Britain and others by France. When I wrote this despatch in 1922 I was advised by, among others, Colonel Lawrence, the truest champion of Arab rights whom modern times have known. He has recorded his opinion that the settlement was fair and just — his definite, settled opinion. Together we placed the Emir Abdulla in Transjordania, where he remains faithful and prosperous to this day. Together, under the responsibility of the Prime

From a speech in Parliament, May 23, 1939.

Minister of those days, King Feisal was placed upon the throne of Iraq, where his descendants now rule. But we also showed ourselves continually resolved to close no door upon the ultimate development of a Jewish National Home, fed by continued Jewish immigration into Palestine.

King Hussein On Arab-Jewish Cooperation

Mr. George Antonius in *The Arab Awakening* (p. 269) refers to an article from "Al Qibla" (Mecca) No. 183, of March 23, 1918, which he says appears to have been written by Hussein himself, "calling upon the Arab population in Palestine to bear in mind that their sacred books and their traditions enjoined upon them the duties of hospitality and tolerance, and exhorting them to welcome the Jews as brethren and co-operate with them for the common welfare."

It should be added that this article also refers to the remarkable achievements of the Jewish people in Palestine as worthy of imitation by the Arabs and states that "the resources of the country are still virgin soil," and will be developed by the labour and capital of the Jewish immigrants. "One of the most amazing things till recent times," the article goes on, "was that the Palestinian used to leave his country, wandering over the high seas in every direction. His native soil could not retain him, though his ancestors had lived on it for over a thousand years. And, at the same time, we saw the Jews from foreign countries streaming to Palestine from Russia, Germany, Austria, Spain, America. * * * The cause of causes could not escape those who had the gift of a deeper insight; they knew that that country was for its original sons (abna'ihi-l-asliyin), for all their differences, a sacred and beloved homeland. Experience has proved their capacity to succeed in their energies and their labours. * * * The return of these exiles (jaliya) to their homeland will prove materially and spiritually an experimental school for their brethren [i.e., the Arabs] who are with them in the fields, factories, trades, and in all things connected with toil and labour."

Hearings before House Committee on Foreign Affairs, February, 1944.

An Adventure in the Human Spirit

Abba Eban

Four thousand years of history have extended their span between Israel's first nationhood and her restoration to freedom at the turning point of this century. The redemption from Egyptian bondage must be regarded in any serious view of history as one of the authentic points of climax in the progress of mankind. In the words of Henry George: "From between the paws of the rock-hewn Sphinx rises the genius of human liberty; and the trumpets of the Exodus throb with the defiant proclamation of the rights of man."

These forceful phrases do not overstate the case. The flight across the Red Sea and Sinai preserved a revolutionary idea, which could never have evolved in the idolatrous despotism of the Pharaohs. The idea was the sovereignty of God, the Ruler of the universe, omnipotent, one and indivisible, the embodiment of righteousness and the loving Father of all creation. From this idea there flowed acceptances and rejections which came to dominate life amongst the children of man. Recognizing this event as the beginning of our true destiny we, the descendants of those fleeing slaves have, in all succeeding generations, commemorated the ancient saga. Our tradition, to this day, exhorts every Jew to recite the story of the Exodus from Egypt at the appointed season as though he personally had experienced this redemption from servitude to freedom.

The narrative of this rebellion against idolatry by men charged with the custody of an idea also occurs in the history of thought in a

From a speech delivered at Notre Dame University on January 11, 1955.

more secular aspect. The Exodus is the original and classic episode of national liberation. The memory of Israel's first struggle for freedom has inspired and consoled many subsequent movements for national independence. When Benjamin Franklin and Thomas Jefferson were consulted on the emblem of the future American Union they suggested that the Seal of the United States should represent the Children of Israel fleeing across the parted waters of the Red Sea on their way to freedom. This portrayal was to be surmounted by the uncannily Hebraic slogan: "Resistance to Tyrants is Obedience to God."

It is not, I think, presumptuous to believe that future generations will keep the memories of Israel's modern revival with a similar reverence and tenacity. This will certainly come to pass in the particular domain of Jewish history. Nothing since the miraculous redemption four thousand years ago can compete in our history with this recent transition from martyrdom to sovereignty, this most sudden ascent from the depths of agony to new peaks of opportunity and pride. The attainment of Israel's independence seven years ago is already much more than a political or secular event in the Jewish consciousness. The date is bound to be numbered amidst the festivals of a people whose other temporal milestones have endured with rare constancy.

I have come to this abode of Christian faith and learning to suggest that Israel's resurgence is an event to be conceived in the highest dimensions of human history. It evokes from the past and may portend for the future a deep lesson on the nature of spiritual impulses. The attention which this event has already received in the thought and writing of our age is itself a proof of some special quality within it. It is evident, however, that if Israel's rebirth comes to have this eternal renown, it will not be because of any material dimensions which belong to it. There is nothing global, or even massive, about the State of Israel in political terms. The territory of our new independence is great in history, but pathetically meagre in geography. True, it is the bridge between the three continents of the ancient world. It looks out over the highway which has marked the migrations and invasions of history's pageant. But in the calculations of the atomic century this is a small and humble piece of earth. The bridge is fragile; the highway is narrow, and in the age of air transportation it no longer obtrudes itself inevitably athwart the paths of conquest and empire.

The population directly affected falls short of two million. Even when we portray this event in its real essence, as a collective climax in the history of the Jewish people, it still remains true that the conscious agents of Israel's revival are but a small fraction of the total human family. Clearly then, if modern Israel is to be regarded as an incident of universal scope, this is because of a stature to be ascribed to it in a completely different dimension. If modern Israel is to have any elements of greatness, then this quality must be vindicated in the spiritual realm.

To say this is not to deny that some of Israel's material achievements are impressive and sometimes deeply moving. The collective survival of the Jewish people is itself a rare event of history. Many other peoples have lost their independence under the heel of invading empires; but no people other than this, having been so engulfed, has shown such a capacity for recuperation as to preserve amidst martyrdom and dispersion all the elements of its union and identity—its language and tradition, its consciousness of attachment to the land of its origin, and the undying hope of eventual restoration. For long centuries this people, whithersoever it wandered, continued to regard its inner life as rooted in a distant land which few could ever hope to see with their own eyes. This connection, which for many generations was an act of mystic faith, became transformed, against all material calculations, into one of the political realities of our age. The banner of a free Israel now flies proudly again in the family of nations from which it had been absent for so many tragic generations.

There is surely something here to arrest the attention of those who study history in terms of national politics and international relations. Nor are these the only achievements which may be accounted remarkable in secular terms. There is the pioneering toil and sacrifice which have transformed the wilderness to a semblance of its ancient fertility. There is the epic of mass immigration which has brought hundreds of thousands of returning newcomers to our shores. There are great efforts, and at times serious results, in the increase of industrial and agricultural resources. There is the formation of a new culture, welding many varied immigrant traditions, tongues and experiences into the tapestry of a distinctive civilization, in the image of the ancient Hebrew past. There is the struggle against the ravages of pestilence and erosion which had debased the physical aspect of our land and degraded its historic reputation as "the perfection of beauty, the joy of the entire earth." There is the adventure of establishing within a region dominated by despotism and autocracy a sanctuary for the democratic way of life and the principles of free government. There are advances in literature, the sciences and arts which without yet reaching the peaks of the ancient revelations, are yet significant and promising in relation to the circumstances of time and of space in which they have been accomplished. Nor can I omit from the positive record of Israel's achievement the struggle for physical security by a small people besieged on all its embattled frontiers by an unyielding and comprehensive hostility. To have achieved so large a volume of international recognition within so brief a time and against such heavy challenge is also among the most notable of Israel's victories.

If, despite all this, we concentrate our gaze upon the spiritual aspects of Israel's achievement and destiny, it is not because we renounce our claim to sympathetic appraisal in political, economic, social, and even military history. But when all is said and done there have been greater battles, more far-reaching economic upheavals, vaster irrigation projects, broader revelations of physical power than those which we have recorded, memorable as they are for us. Moreover, even these achievements by Israel, while being political, economic or social in their outward aspect, are primarily significant as illustrations of spiritual forces. They are testimony to the power of the human will. A few decades ago the prospect that an independent Jewish state could be established in its ancient homeland appeared so fantastic as to bring its advocates under suspicion of insanity. Statesmen and diplomats to whom the idea was broached in the early years of the First World War were startled at hearing so eccentric an idea even submitted to their official attention. A British Ambassador in Paris to whom our first President, Dr. Chaim Weizmann, summarized this project in 1915 wrote in his diary that he had encountered a remarkable contradiction—a man of eminent scientific attainments with a keen power of rational analysis who, on this particular issue, appeared to have gone completely off his head. Back in London, Prime Minister Asquith expressed surprise that one of his cabinet colleagues of Jewish faith, normally a man of excessive rationalism, was afflicted with delirium on this special point.

Today, with the third Jewish commonwealth in tangible existence, it is the skeptics and the rationalists who appear incongruous to our eyes. Yet their skepticism seemed then to rest on strong foundations. After all, the Jewish people was dispersed and divided, split up into divergent fragments, lacking any element of political unity. The greater part of them dwelt thousands of miles away from the prospective scene of their national revival. The land itself appeared to have been sucked dry of all its vitality and to offer no prospect of resettlement. Moreover, it was neither empty nor available. It was controlled by strong nationalisms and imperialisms and coveted by others, all of which had a stronger chance of possession than had a dispersed and politically anonymous people. The concept of a Jewish nationhood or indeed of any special link between the Jewish people and its original homeland was completely unrecognized in the jurisprudence of nations. It seemed unlikely that the Zionist program could possibly overcome such hostilities and natural adversities.

Yet within a single lifetime we have passed from a world in which the existence of an independent Israel seemed inconceivable into a world which seems inconceivable without its existence.

I know of few more tangible testimonies in history to the power of the human will to assert itself against material odds. This is the primary value of Israel's rebirth to all those who are concerned with the vindication of faith against the fatalistic or deterministic theories of history, which see the human being not as the primary agent of historic processes but merely as their helpless subject matter. Thus, quite apart from its context in the annals of the Jewish people, the rebirth of modern Israel would earn its place in history as a crushing argument in the eternal discussion between the claims of faith, and the doctrines which deny the human will any central part in governing the world's destiny. Those materialistic doctrines would have an impossible task to perform to explain Israel's revival solely in material or economic terms.

Now this belief in the power of the human will is a recurrent theme in Israel's history. The most distinctive attribute of Israel's character, the source of some weakness but of greater strength is this tenacious refusal to recognize the distinction between imagination and reality. In the grammar of classical Hebrew there is none of the sharp differentiation possessed by modern languages between that which is and that which shall be. This deliberate confusion between imagination and reality, between the will and the fact, has been illustrated at many stages of our history. . .

The aspects of this revival which belong ostensibly to political history, cannot be denied their place in a spiritual appraisal. The homelessness and martyrdom of the Jewish people was not merely a source of Jewish grief and of international political tension; it was also a burden upon the Christian conscience. The weight of this burden became heavy beyond endurance in the aftermath of the Second World War, when the curtain went up on the burnt and mangled bodies of six million Jews, including a million children. The Jewish people had fallen victim to the most fearful agony which had ever beset any family of the human race. A whole continent was saturated with its blood and haunted by its unexpiated sacrifice. As the world rose from the ravages of the Second World War, it came perilously near to creating an injustice more heinous than any which had been eliminated by the triumph of the Allied cause. It became horribly but seriously possible that every nation would be granted its freedom, amongst those which had suffered under the heel of tyranny, except the people which had suffered the most. All the victims of tyranny would be established in sovereignty, except the first and the most sorely ravaged amongst the targets of totalitarian persecution. If the world order had been established under Christian leadership upon this discrimination, it would surely have been conceived with an intolerable measure of original guilt.

From this spiritual peril the community of nations cleansed itself belatedly, perhaps a little too grudgingly, but nevertheless decisively, when it ordained and later recognized the establishment of Israel. An international society including a Jewish State, and an international society after the Second World War excluding any satisfaction of the Jewish claim to equality, would have been two totally antithetical concepts from the ethical point of view. Thus the renewal of Israel's sovereignty, though ostensibly a fact of political organization was, in the deeper sense, an act of universal equity. It is a stage of preferment in the history of the Christian conscience.

The same consideration applies with particular force when we examine the problem of equity in its regional aspect. No people benefited more lavishly than the Arabs from the new inheritance of freedom bequeathed by the victories of the Allied powers in two World Wars and the establishment of the United Nations. In an area where not a single free Arab or Moslem had lived in political independence four decades ago, there were now to be created seven, eight and then nine separate Arab sovereignties extending over a vast sub-continent from Pakistan to the Central Mediterranean, from the Taurus mountains to the Persian Gulf. This region of Arab independence was immeasurably rich in physical power. Great fertile valleys spread out within it. Abundant rivers flowed across its lands. Unlimited resources of mineral and natural wealth lay beneath its soil. Never since the great era of the Moslem Caliphate, a full millennium ago, had the Arab world commanded such elements of strength and opportunity as those which now came within its reach.

Here again the international conscience was faced with a burning problem of equity. Would it be considered right for the Arab people to hold sway over a vast continent, and wrong for the Jewish people to establish its independence in a mere fragment of this huge domain? Would it be the decree of history that the Arabs must be independent everywhere and the Jewish people nowhere—not even in the land which owed all its renown in history to its connection with the Hebrew tradition? This was the problem of conscience which underlay those political discussions in international forums and in the chancelleries of the powers. Here again there was the peril of an award so one-sided and discriminatory as to weigh down the international conscience for generations to come. After many hesitations the world community purged itself of any such reproach. It rightly established and encouraged the emancipation of the Arab people on an almost imperial scale. But the benefit, nay the elementary right, which it conferred upon the Arabs in such abundance was also bestowed upon the Jewish people, albeit within more meagre and austere limits. This picture of an Arab freedom beyond the wildest dreams of recent generations, side by side with an immeasurably more modest satisfaction of the principle of Jewish independence should stand before us whenever we consider the spiritual implications of the controversy between Arab and Israel nationalism. It would have been an indelible disgrace to universal justice if a world which had rightly bequeathed this vast liberation to the Arab nations had begrudged the Jewish people its small share of freedom.

"Our Jewish Pilgrim Fathers"

Louis D. Brandeis

Let us bear clearly in mind what Zionism is, or rather what it is not.

It is not a movement to remove all the Jews of the world compulsorily to Palestine. In the first place there are 14,000,000 Jews, and Palestine would not accommodate more than one-third of that number. In the second place, it is not a movement to compel anyone to go to Palestine. It is essentially a movement to give to the Jew more, not less freedom — it aims to enable the Jews to exercise the same right now exercised by practically every other people in the world: To live at their option either in the land of their fathers or in some other country; a right which members of small nations as well as of large,—which Irish, Greek, Bulgarian, Serbian, or Belgian, may now exercise as fully as Germans or English.

Zionism seeks to establish in Palestine, for such Jews as choose to go and remain there, and for their descendants, a legally secured home, where they may live together and lead a Jewish life, where they may expect ultimately to constitute a majority of the population, and may look forward to what we should call home rule. The Zionists seek to establish this home in Palestine because they are convinced that the undying longing of Jews for Palestine is a fact of deepest significance; that it is a manifestation in the struggle for existence by an ancient people which had established its right to live—a people whose three thousand years of civilization has produced a faith, culture and individuality which enable them to con-

From "The Jewish Problem and How to Solve It," 1915.

tribute largely in the future as they had in the past to the advance of civilization and that it is not a right merely but a duty of the Jewish nationality to survive and develop. They believe that there only, can Jewish life be fully protected from the forces of disintegration; that there alone, can the Jewish spirit reach its full and natural development; and that by securing for those Jews who wish to settle in Palestine, the opportunity to do so, not only those Jews, but all other Jews will be benefited and that the long perplexing Jewish Problem will, at last, find solution.

They believe that to accomplish this, it is not necessary that the Jewish population of Palestine be large as compared with the whole number of Jews in the world; for throughout centuries when the Jewish influence was greatest,—during the Persian, the Greek, and the Roman Empires, only a relatively small part of the Jews lived in Palestine; and only a small part of the Jews returned from Babylon when the Temple was rebuilt.

Since the destruction of the Temple, nearly two thousand years ago, the longing for Palestine has been ever present with the Jew. It was the hope of a return to the land of his fathers that buoyed up the Jew amidst persecution, and for the realization of which the devout ever prayed. Until a generation ago this was a hope merely—a wish piously prayed for, but not worked for. The Zionist movement is idealistic, but it is also essentially practical. It seeks to realize that hope; to make the dream of a Jewish life in a Jewish land come true as other great dreams of the world have been realized—by men working with devotion, intelligence, and self-sacrifice. It was thus that the dream of Italian independence and unity, after centuries of vain hope, came true through the efforts of Mazzini, Garibaldi and Cavour; that the dream of Greek, of Bulgarian and of Serbian independence became facts; that the dream of home rule in Ireland had just been realized.

The rebirth of the Jewish nation is no longer a mere dream. It is in process of accomplishment in a most practical way, and the story is a wonderful one. A generation ago a few Jewish emigrants from Russia and from Roumania, instead of proceeding westward to this hospitable country where they might easily have secured material prosperity, turned eastward for the purpose of settling in the land of their fathers.

To the worldly wise these efforts at colonization appeared very foolish. Nature and man presented obstacles in Palestine which appeared almost insuperable; and the colonists were in fact ill-equipped for their task, save in their spirit of devotion and self-sacrifice. The land, harassed by centuries of misrule, was treeless and apparently sterile; and it was infested with malaria. The Government offered them no security, either as to life or property. The colonists themselves were not only unfamiliar with the character of the country, but were ignorant of the farmer's life which they proposed to lead; for the Jews of Russia and Roumania had been generally denied the opportunity of owning or working land. Furthermore, these colonists were not inured to the physical hardships to which the life of a pioneer is necessarily subjected. To these hardships and malaria many succumbed. Those who survived were long confronted with failure. But at last success came. Within a generation these Jewish Pilgrim Fathers, and those who followed them, have succeeded in establishing these two fundamental propositions:

First: That Palestine is fit for the modern Jew.

Second: That the modern Jew is fit for Palestine.

Over forty self-governing Jewish colonies attested to this remarkable achievement.

This land, treeless a generation ago, supposed to be sterile and hopelessly arid, has been shown to have been treeless and sterile only because of man's misrule. It has been shown to be capable of becoming again a land "flowing with milk and honey." Oranges and grapes, olives and almonds, wheat and other cereals are now growing there in profusion.

This material development has been attended by a spiritual and social development no less extraordinary; a development in education, in health and in social order; and in the character and habits of the population. Perhaps the most extraordinary achievement of Jewish nationalism is the revival of the Hebrew Language, which has again become a language of the common intercourse of men. The Hebrew tongue, called a dead language for nearly two thousand years, has, in the Jewish colonies and in Jerusalem, become again the living mother tongue. The effect of this common language in unifying the Jew is, of course, great; for the Jews of Palestine came literally from all the lands of the earth, each speaking, except for the use of Yiddish, the language of the country from which he came, and remaining in the main, almost a stranger to the others. But the effect of the renaissance of the Hebrew tongue is far greater than that of unifying the Jews. It is a potent factor in reviving the essentially Jewish spirit.

Our Jewish Pilgrim Fathers have laid the foundation. It remains for us to build the superstructure.

Let no American imagine that Zionism is inconsistent with Patriotism. Multiple loyalties are objectionable only if they are inconsistent. A man is a better citizen of the United States for being a loyal citizen of his state, and of his city; for being loyal to his family, and to his profession or trade; for being loyal to his college or his lodge. Every Irish-American who contributed towards advancing home rule was a better man and a better American for the sacrifice he made. Every American Jew who aids in advancing the Jewish settlement in Palestine, though he feels that neither he nor his descendants will ever live there, will likewise be a better man and a better American for doing so.

Note what Seton-Watson says:

"America is full of nationalities which, while accepting with enthusiasm their new American citizenship, nevertheless look to some centre in the old world as the source and inspiration of their national culture and traditions. The most typical instance is the feeling of the American Jew for Palestine which may well become a focus for his *declasse* kinsmen in other parts of the world."

There is no inconsistency between loyalty to America and loyalty to Jewry. The Jewish spirit, the product of our religion and experiences, is essentially modern and essentially American. Not since the destruction of the Temple have the Jews in spirit and in ideals been so fully in harmony with the noblest aspirations of the country in which they lived.

America's fundamental law seeks to make real the brotherhood of man. That brotherhood became the Jewish fundamental law more than twenty-five hundred years ago. America's insistent demand in the twentieth century is for social justice. That also has been the Jews' striving for ages. Their affliction as well as their religion has prepared the Jews for effective democracy. Persecution broadened their sympathies. It trained them in patient endurance, in self-control, and in sacrifice. It made them think as well as suffer. It deepened the passion for righteousness.

Indeed, loyalty to America demands rather that each American Jew become a Zionist. For only through the ennobling effect of its strivings can we develop the best that is in us and give to this country the full benefit of our great inheritance. The Jewish spirit, so long preserved, the character developed by so many centuries of sacrifice, should be preserved and developed further, so that in America as elsewhere the sons of the race, may in future live lives and do deeds worthy of their ancestors.

From Israel's Proclamation of Independence

The State of Israel will be open to Jewish immigration and the ingathering of exiles. It will devote itself to developing the Land for the good of all its inhabitants.

It will rest upon foundations of liberty, justice and peace as envisioned by the Prophets of Israel. It will maintain complete equality of social and political rights for all its citizens, without distinction of creed, race or sex. It will guarantee freedom of religion and conscience, of language, education and culture. It will safeguard the Holy Places of all religions. It will be loyal to the principles of the United Nations Charter. . .

Even amidst the violent attacks launched against us for months past, we call upon the sons of the Arab people dwelling in Israel to keep the peace and to play their part in building the State on the basis of full and equal citizenship and due representation in all its institutions, provisional and permanent.

We extend the hand of peace and good-neighbourliness to all the States around us and to their peoples, and we call upon them to cooperate in mutual helpfulness with the independent Jewish nation in its Land. The State of Israel is prepared to make its contribution in a concerted effort for the advancement of the entire Middle East.

Tel Aviv, May 14, 1948

Israel in Search of Peace

Golda Meir

Twenty-five years ago the Jewish state proclaimed its independence in a part of Palestine. Six months earlier, the General Assembly of the United Nations had recommended its establishment. This act of historic justice strove to fulfill the earlier pledge of the Balfour Declaration and the League of Nations Mandate which gave recognition not only to an immediate Jewish need but also to the principle of a Jewish right to national self-expression. Zionism, as an aspiration, is as old as the Exile. As a political movement it goes back a hundred years. The vision of a Jewish return to the original homeland is far older than the solemn international commitments of 25 and 55 years ago. An independent Jewish state arose as the culmination of a long process of national liberation, which eventually won formal sanction through the moral sense of the community of nations.

In the twenty-fifth year of independence, Israel has ample cause for satisfaction: she has developed from a community of 600,000 at the close of the British Mandate into a technologically advanced, democratic state of three million. She has fulfilled her mission of homeland and refuge by absorbing over a million Jews from every sector of the globe, including half a million refugees from Arab lands as well as hundreds of thousands of survivors of the Nazi holocaust; and while engaged in her enormous constructive tasks she has managed, though vastly outnumbered, to repel concerted assaults by the Arab states on her very life. She has translated a remote

Reprinted by permission from Foreign Affairs, *April, 1973. Copyright 1973 by Council on Foreign Relations, Inc.*

dream into solid reality. In all this Israel has brought to fruition the labor of Jewish pioneers who, since the turn of the century, gave their lives to transform a barren and denuded land into fertile fields, flourishing settlements and new patterns of society. In surveying the burgeoning towns of modern Israel, it is easy to forget that the land to which the young settlers came was rich only in historic memories and religious associations. It had neither oil nor abundant natural resources. Its wastes offered no temptation except to Zionist pioneers animated by the twin ideals of a new Jewish society and a reconstructed land.

The renewal of Jewish national independence after centuries of dispersion and persecution is one of the great ethical affirmations of our time. An age-old inequity was at last redressed, not at the expense of another people, but with full regard for the rights of others. For we were not alone in securing independence. In a parallel development, many Arab states were established in the same period and in the same region but in a far more generous expanse. In the huge area liberated by the Allies from Turkish domination we had been accorded a "small notch" which we sought to develop in peace and cooperation with our neighbors. The failure of that hope has been costly to both Arab and Jew, and I shall not pretend that the persistent conflict with the Arabs does not weigh heavily upon us.

Decades of struggle have brought much bloodshed to both. Nothing can be more horrifying than parents burying their children, and I know of families who have lost three generations of their sons in this tragic conflict. We would be happier if we could use all our energy in the more rewarding tasks of reclaiming the deserts and bare hills which still constitute so much of Israel. In Israel, as elsewhere, there are problems of economic deprivation and social maladjustment whose solution would be hastened by peace. But peace still remains elusive. Though the Arab peoples suffer grave ills of poverty and disease, their governments concentrate mainly on the sterile goal of destroying Israel's independence. This fixation torments the Middle East and obstructs its creative destiny.

II

Yet this grim course was not inevitable. The heart of the Zionist faith was the conviction that Jewish independence could be achieved in harmony with Arab national aspirations.

From its inception, Zionism, as a political movement, strove to establish an Arab-Jewish understanding. A great number of attempts had been made before the famous Weizmann-Faisal agreement of January 1919 which welcomed the Jews to Palestine. These were followed by attempts in the 1930s and 1940s. All had one aim in view: to reach an agreement with our Arab neighbors. As late as 1947-48, we tried, in vain, to avert the course of events. In November 1947, shortly before the Partition Resolution was adopted at the United Nations, King Abdullah of Jordan promised me that he would never join the Arab states in a war against us and that after the U.N. Resolution was adopted we would meet to work out ways and means of peace and co-operation between our states. As late as May 10, 1948, just five days before the British were to leave Palestine, I crossed into what was already enemy territory — Jordan — and met the King in Amman. As I drove on the road leading to Amman, I could see the Mafraq camp and the Iraqi troops and guns massing there. At that meeting, King Abdullah did not deny the promise given me in November, but he stated that if we declared ourselves a state and insisted on unlimited Jewish immigration, he would have no choice but to join in a war against us. His alternative was to bring the whole area under his domination and curtail Jewish immigration. That was 25 years ago. Since the achievement of our independence and the conclusion of the Armistice Agreements of 1949, we have left no stone unturned in an endless effort to find avenues of dialogue which might lead to agreement.

Nothing could be more false than the Arab script in which Zionist "aggressors" appeared on the scene to dispossess local Palestinians. Since this accusation still constitutes the burden of the Arab case and provides the rationale for Arab enmity, it cannot be ignored even though the answers, like the charges, are familiar. We cannot assume a guilt we do not feel for sufferings of which we were not the cause.

Let me put it in the simplest terms. When I came to Palestine in 1921 my pioneer generation was neither morally obtuse nor uninformed. We knew there were Arabs in Palestine, just as we knew from our own experience that our labor in malaria-ridden kibbutzim transformed uninhabitable swamps into habitable soil. Far from ignoring the local population, we were sustained by the sincere conviction that our toil created more and better living space for both Arab and Jew. In this belief we were proven right. Between 1922 and 1947, the Arab population of Palestine grew from 670,000 to

1,200,000 — a spectacular increase paralleled in no neighboring Arab territory. Thanks to the agricultural and industrial development of the country, Palestine changed from a land of Arab emigration to one of Arab immigration attracted by the higher standards of living and greater opportunities. The supposed Zionist dispossession of Arabs is a myth disproven by every official census.

We were also fully aware of Arab national aspirations in the Middle East. We assumed that these aspirations would find ample satisfaction in the various Arab states set up by the Allies in the vast areas freed from Ottoman domination. By the end of the British Mandate, 99 percent of that area had been allotted to the Arabs, one percent to the Jewish homeland. If there was any inequity in this distribution, surely the Arabs were not its victims. Hence we hoped, sincerely if perhaps naïvely, that Jewish and Arab independence would flourish peacefully side by side to the advantage of the entire Middle East.

Something else should be made clear. Palestinian Arab nationalism was not a visible factor at the time. Until recently, Arab nationalism constantly opposed the designation of one sector of the Middle East as Palestine. It regarded this "particularism" as a violation of the concept of a unitary Arab state. The territory that Jews cherished as historic Palestine the Arabs viewed merely as Southern Syria. As late as 1956, Ahmed Shukairy, at that time Syrian representative to the United Nations and later head of the Palestine Liberation Organization, declared in the Security Council that "it is common knowledge that Palestine is nothing but Southern Syria."

At the time of the rebirth of the Jewish state, the argument was between the Jewish people and the Arab people. Though the nationalist demands of the latter had been richly fulfilled, they refused to honor the equivalent legitimacy of Jewish rights. Their position was that Arabs should be sovereign everywhere, the Jews nowhere.

Thus it was Arab intransigence that led to the compromise of the U.N. Partition Resolution by which the area encompassed by the Balfour Declaration was further cut so that Israel arose in one-fifth of the territory originally allotted for a Jewish homeland. (The first truncation had taken place in 1922 when three-fourths of the original Palestine area was severed for the establishment of Transjordan.) Nevertheless, for the sake of independence, peace and the possibility of freely bringing Jewish survivors to Israel's shores, the Jews accepted this compromise and created Israel in a spirit of joy and hope. Instead of the Arabs doing likewise and establishing their state in the area assigned to them by the U.N. Resolution, seven Arab states attacked new-born Israel. They refused to accept the existence of the Jewish state and sought to throttle it at birth.

III

This chronology is essential for an understanding of the present impasse. There can be no greater mistake in assessing the current situation in the Middle East than to assume that the conflict continues because of a specific political Arab grievance: the plight of the Arab refugees; the Israeli presence on the West Bank, or in the Sinai; the reunification of Jerusalem. The record bears out the error of this view. In 1947-48, when seven Arab states launched the invasion which resulted in the exodus of 600,000 Arabs, mainly to other parts of Palestine — to the West Bank, Gaza and Jordan — there had been no dispossessed Arabs and no Arab refugees. The Arab refugee problem was the result, not the cause, of the 1948 war. In June 1967, Sinai, Gaza, the West Bank, the Golan Heights and East Jerusalem were all in Arab possession. Nevertheless, the Arabs concentrated their troops in Sinai, established a blockade and announced, in Nasser's words on May 27, 1967, that the object of the war was "the destruction of Israel." It is therefore absurd to contend that the present territorial configuration is the cause of the Middle East tension.

The heart of the problem is what caused the Six Day War, not the territories administered by Israel after the war. Simply put, the root issue is the Arab attitude to Israel's very existence and security. Once the Arab countries accept the legitimacy of Israel as we have always accepted theirs, there is no reason for their intransigence against negotiating the differences between us. In this connection, let me state as firmly as I can that Israel's insistence on negotiations, direct or indirect, is not a maneuver devised to bait our Arab enemies. The vehement refusal of the Arab leaders to discuss with us the terms of a peace settlement must raise the question as to whether they are really prepared to live in peace with us. This is the crux of the conflict.

Israel is sometimes accused of "rigidity" in her stated positions and is exhorted to be more "flexible." These charges deserve careful examination. Since 1967, we have shifted from our original demand for direct bilateral negotiations — which we consider the most effective and promising method — to a procedure similar to that employed at Rhodes in 1948-49, when talks, both direct and indirect, took place. In 1970, in order to meet Arab intransigence, we agreed to the procedure of indirect negotiation in the first stage, hoping that this would pave the road to a peace agreement. An even more fundamental indication of Israel's readiness for compromise may be found in our policy statements. We have said that whereas Israel would not return to the tragically vulnerable pre-June 1967 armistice lines, we do not insist that the present ceasefire lines be final. We thus leave open a very broad area for meaningful negotiation and compromise. The Arab states, on the other hand, continue to reiterate their demand for Israel's "total withdrawal" to the June 4, 1967 lines. By this demand they distort Security Council Resolution 242 which never called for total withdrawal, or withdrawal from all the territories. The language of the Resolution is withdrawal "from territories," acknowledging Israel's right to live within "secure and recognized boundaries." All attempts made to insert in the Resolution the demand for total withdrawal or withdrawal from "the" territories were rejected by the Security Council.

We know that the phrase "secure and recognized boundaries" is not a magic incantation. It is a theme for negotiation. In our insistence on this point, we are motivated by two realistic considerations based on our experience since 1948. We want boundaries whose very character will make aggression less inviting to any would-be invader, and which could be defended with fewer casualties if such aggression nevertheless took place. The enormous advantages in size of population and topography which our adversaries have always enjoyed have tempted them periodically to make assaults upon us. We want to weaken such temptation to the greatest possible degree.

After three wars for survival in the last 25 years, we cannot reasonably be expected to disregard our bitter experience. In 1948, 1956 and 1967, we learned how swiftly Egypt could move her tanks and regiments into Sinai from the south, and how readily our southern maritime approach could be blockaded from Sharm-el-Sheikh. To the south stretched the Gaza Strip, pointing as an aggressive finger into the heart of our territory. From there, fedayeen regularly infiltrated and carried out sabotage and murder, reaching all the way to the outskirts of Tel Aviv. On the eastern border

Jordanian guns, pointing at our dwellings, could be seen by our children playing in the streets of Jerusalem. The city could be bombarded from our very doorstep. Israel herself could be readily cut at her 12-mile waist between the old line with Jordan and the sea near Nethanya. In the north, from the fortified ridge of the Golan Heights, the Syrians shelled our kibbutzim in the valley at will. To the west lay the Mediterranean into which the Arabs regularly promised to drive us. Having escaped from such tight encirclement, we feel justified in our determination not to reënter again a trap composed of vulnerable geography. Even in an age of rockets and missiles, we cannot renounce the added security inherent in more rational boundaries which would keep the potential adversary at a greater distance from our homes. When the new European security system was established after the Second World War, no one in his right mind proposed the precise reconstruction of the map which had spelled vulnerability and disaster for so many nations.

The border changes Israel seeks do not involve loss of territory vital to Arab interests. The Sinai desert has in the past served no Egyptian purpose save to provide a ready staging-ground for attacks on Israel and for the maintenance of blockade. No Egyptians live in Sinai and only a few Bedouin tribes (not Egyptian citizens) roam its sands. Sharm-el-Sheikh, a desolate, uninhabited outpost, was used by the Egyptians only to blockade the Gulf of Aqaba. In any case, Israel, under a peace settlement, would not seek to retain all or most of Sinai. As for the Golan Heights, it constituted primarily a military fortress directed at our agricultural settlements in the valley below. The West Bank presents a more complex problem. I have made it clear several times that in negotiations with the Kingdom of Jordan we will naturally present proposals for a territorial agreement.

My general comment holds good: the border changes sought by Israel will, by reducing the strategic advantage enjoyed by a would-be aggressor, help to deter war. Conversely, reconstructing these advantages would facilitate hostile designs against Israel and renew the prospects of war.

This is not the first time in our history that Israel has been urged to withdraw from Sinai, Sharm-el-Sheikh and Gaza at the close of hostilities: In 1956, in response to the massing of Egyptian armor in Sinai, the blockade of the Straits of Tiran, and the terrorist incursions from Egyptian-held Gaza, Israel acted in the Sinai. We repelled the Egyptian army, freed the Gaza Strip occupied by Egypt in 1948, removed Egyptian gun-emplacements that for six years had blockaded the Gulf of Aqaba, and restored free access for the movement of ships through a waterway which has the character of a lifeline for Israel.

In response to solemn assurances that the blockade would not be renewed, terrorist infiltration would not be restored, and the Egyptian forces would not reënter Gaza, Israel agreed to withdraw from Sinai, Sharm-el-Sheikh and Gaza. As Foreign Minister, it was my office in March 1957 to announce to the General Assembly Israel's compliance with the U.N. Resolution calling for such withdrawal. Previously (January 1957), I had warned the General Assembly of the consequences of any action that might result "in the restoration of the blockade, and the consequent renewal of regional conflict, and international tension." And I asked, in words painfully relevant today: "Shall Egypt be allowed once more to organize murder and sabotage in this strip [Gaza]? Shall Egypt be allowed to condemn the local population to permanent impoverishment and to block any solution of the refugee problem?"

The world knows what happened. Despite the "assurances" and the "hopes and expectations" on the strength of which Israel withdrew, Egyptian troops promptly reoccupied Gaza. Learning of this betrayal of our good faith as soon as I got back to Israel, I at once returned to the United States to voice my indignation to Secretary of State Dulles and U.N. Secretary-General Hammarskjöld. I shall never forget Secretary Hammarskjöld's blunt question: "It's not worth going to war for again, is it?" In 1967, the remaining elements of the 1957 arrangements were unilaterally violated by Egypt.

The repeated failure of international arrangements to safeguard our country's vital interests has taught us a lesson we do not easily forget. International decisions proved meaningless in each crisis that we faced: in 1948 when the Arab states violated the Partition Resolution; in the long years of lawless blockade and terrorist incursion; and in 1967 when the international community, which had "assured" our territorial integrity and freedom from blockade, proved powerless to stand by its commitments. Hence, we inevitably reflect on this history when urged to take action which could result in diminishing our capacity for self-defense and make us dependent on international guarantees.

History repeats itself in the Middle East. After every war staged by the Arab states against us, they demand the restoration of the very borders they set out to destroy. When Egypt insists now upon total withdrawal of Israeli forces to the pre-June 4, 1967 lines, the simple question arises: If those borders were so sanctified for Egypt after the war, why were they not honored by Egypt before the war and why launch war to destroy them in the first place? The bitter truth is that the Arab leaders have not changed their attitudes about our very presence in this area. Arab statesmen, from Nasser to Sadat, have made no secret of their proposed strategy. Mohamed Hassanein Heikal, the influential editor of the Egyptian daily, *Al-Ahram*, formulated a notorious "Theory of Two Stages" in an article on February 25, 1971:

> There are only two specific Arab goals at present: elimination of the consequences of the 1967 aggression through Israel's withdrawal from all the lands it occupied that year, and elimination of the consequences of the 1948 aggression through the eradication of Israel.
>
> The second goal is not, in fact, specific but abstract, and some of us make the mistake of starting with the second step instead of the first. On the basis of the conditions I have mentioned, it is possible to believe in the possibility of attaining the first goal. As for the second goal, we should learn from the enemy how to move step by step. [1]

We find this strategy all too concrete and decline to facilitate its implementation. Israel is a democracy in which various views, minimalist and maximalist, are freely advocated. We have our doves and hawks. Most Israelis are neither, but we do refuse the role of clay pigeon. More than once I have made it clear that we are ready for negotiations on the issue of borders and that we have never said that the ceasefire lines have to be the peace boundaries on all sectors. The borders must be defensible and for that purpose significant changes in the previous lines are necessary, but we are ready for a territorial compromise.

IV

Jerusalem, mourned in Jewish prayers since the fall of the Temple, was never without a community ot pious Jews. Furthermore, Jews constituted a majority of the ancient city from the mid-nineteenth century until 1948, when the Jordanian Army seized the eastern half of Jerusalem, including the walled Old City with its religious shrines sacred to Jews, Muslims and Christians, and drove out the Jewish inhabitants.

---

[1] Cairo Radio, February 26, 1971, quoted from BBC Monitoring Service.

According to the 1949 Armistice Agreements signed by Jordan and Israel, free access to the Jewish Holy Places, to the Mount of Olives and to the university and hospital on Mount Scopus was agreed to. But instead of honoring this commitment, Jordan divided the city with walls, barbed wire and gun emplacements. For the first time since the Roman conquest, Jews were prevented from praying at their holiest shrine, the Western Wall. During the 19 years of Jordanian occupation, Jews were barred from their religious sites in total violation of the Armistice Agreements. Israel's repeated appeals to the Security Council brought no redress.

In June 1967, Jordan again began shelling Jerusalem despite Israel's message to King Hussein, sent through General Odd Bull, the U.N. representative, that Israel would not attack if Jordan kept out of the conflict. Hussein joined the Egyptian assault with the result that Jordan lost her hold on eastern Jerusalem. Israel reunited the artificially rent city. Our joy in the liberation of Jerusalem was marred by the sight of the sacred ancient Jewish Quarter and the venerable synagogues destroyed by Jordan. The Jewish cemetery on the Mount of Olives had been desecrated and thousands of its tombstones used as paving stones for Jordanian roads. Since 1967, Jews, Christians and Muslims have moved freely in and out of all its sectors.

Perhaps this record will explain why we view fears that are sometimes expressed for the sanctity of Jerusalem under Israeli rule as disingenuous. In 1948 and in 1967 the Arabs shelled Jerusalem with no regard for the safety of churches and holy places, without rousing the vocal apprehension of the world. In 1967, Israeli soldiers, to spare Jerusalem, risked their lives in hand-to-hand fighting, street by narrow street, rather than resort to heavy armor. Jordanian troops, on the other hand, used church roofs and even the minarets of their own mosques for gun emplacements. Journalists covering the Six Day War commented on the reverence with which Israeli soldiers approached Jerusalem.

Since that time, satisfaction has been expressed by Christian dignitaries at the care which Israel has bestowed on the Holy Places of Christendom. We have also shown strict regard for Muslim sanctuaries, though, while rebuilding our ruined synagogues and devastated Jewish Quarter, we have had cause to regret that the Arabs failed to display an equivalent respect for what we hold dear.

Israel has publicly announced her policy that Christian and Muslim Holy Places be administered by the respective heads of these religions. To this end, Israel wishes to enter into special agreements with the heads of the various denominations for the detailed implementation of this policy. Jerusalem shall remain united and the capital of Israel. Its Arab inhabitants will, of course, continue to enjoy full freedom and equality.

I don't find it necessary to refute Arab propaganda about Israel's alleged ill-treatment of the local population of the West Bank and the Gaza Strip. Such charges are readily disproven by the daily life of the areas, the success of the "open bridges" policy, and the testimony of impartial observers. The manifest material advantages of the Arab inhabitants of the West Bank and Gaza are undisputed. I know that a marked rise in the standard of living, free opportunities for work at the Israeli wage-rate (which is twice as high as Jordan's), and the introduction of modern health and technological services are welcome benefits, but they do not in themselves solve sensitive political and national issues.

Let me therefore return to the overriding question of peace. In his recent article in *Foreign Affairs*,[2] President Sadat, among other accusations, several times charges that Israel seeks to "dominate" the Middle East. It is hard for me to believe that an Arab statesman seriously believes this evil phantasy. But Voltaire's epigram — as long as men believe absurdities they will commit atrocities — reminds us of the bloody persecutions and wars that have stained the course of human history because men believed absurdities about others. The carnage of the Nazi epoch is only the most terrifying example of the depth to which people sink through the acceptance of imbecilic myths. For this reason I stress the obvious.

We are a small people of some three million among a hundred million Arabs, as our adversaries never tire of reminding us. A glance at the map shows Israel as a mere pinpoint amid huge Arab territories. To suggest that Israel, no matter how able or energetic, seeks to "dominate" this vast expanse is of the stuff of the "Elders of Zion" forgery, according to which the tiny persecuted Jewish minority conspired to rule the world.

Let me review our record in the Middle East. Though the Balfour Declaration promised a Jewish homeland in the area of historic Palestine — an area extending from the Mediterranean to the bor-

---

[2]*Anwar el-Sadat, "Where Egypt Stands,"* Foreign Affairs, *October 1972.*

ders of present-day Iraq — we accepted the severance of three-fourths of that territory for the establishment of the Hashemite Kingdom east of the Jordan. We later accepted the further shrinkage of the original pledge through the U.N. Partition Resolution. Still later, in the tense last week of May 1967, when the Arab onslaught was imminent, Prime Minister Eshkol turned to the Arab states with a final plea for peace: "I would like to say again to the Arab countries, particularly Egypt and Syria, that we harbor no aggressive designs. We have no possible interest in violating either their security, their territory or their legitimate rights." The Arabs responded by proclaiming that the hour of Israel's annihilation had struck.

We did not seek to "expand" but neither did we dismiss Arab threats of a holocaust as "rhetoric." We are too aware of the disparity of forces and resources available to Arab states for us to discount promises the Arabs twice before tried to fulfill. Having been driven to defend ourselves, we secured the bridgeheads from which our enemies sought to destroy us, but successful self-defense is hardly evidence of a desire for "domination." Survival is not aggression.

In his article, President Sadat dwells on the impropriety of keeping "the fruits of victory." I do not care to speculate on what would have been the fate of Israel had the Arabs enjoyed those fruits. Nor am I aware of any modern country that waged a successful war of self-defense whose peace treaty failed to correct the vulnerable and dangerous positions which had made it an inviting target for aggression. The adjustment of the border between Poland and East Germany provides a contemporary instance of significant border changes involving large areas of populated territory with the aim of offering increased security.

Israel is convinced that Poland was justified in insisting upon this territorial adjustment, and Chancellor Brandt is evidence that this is the sentiment of world opinion generally. Anyone familiar with our region cannot reasonably suggest that our right to insist upon border changes is less than that of Poland.

V

Total peace would be a more constructive slogan than total withdrawal. Since it may not be possible to reach total peace in a single step, Israel is willing to negotiate the immediate settlement of specific issues, notably that affecting the reopening of the Suez Canal. We have made the following proposal in regard to the Suez

Canal: "With a view to facilitating the attainment of durable peace between Israel and the U.A.R., Israel is prepared to consider entering into a Special Agreement with the U.A.R. for the opening of the Suez Canal to international navigation, the observance of a ceasefire without limitation of time and nonresumption of fighting, and the stationing of the Israel Defense Forces [IDF] at some distance east of the Suez Canal."

Among particulars spelled out in this proposal, the suggested agreement calls for the release of all prisoners of war within 15 days of its signing. It also states that the line to which the IDF would withdraw east of the Canal would not be considered final; subsequently the IDF would withdraw to the boundary determined by a peace settlement.

In offering, before a final peace, to forgo the strategic advantage of the water barrier provided by the Suez Canal, Israel took a calculated risk as a step toward the relaxation of tension. Such a decisive concession is hardly evidence of an intractable disposition. Of the countries involved, Israel has the least to gain from the Canal; Egypt the most. Yet Egypt rejected the proposal. Egypt demands an Israeli commitment to withdraw to the June 4, 1967 lines, prior to any process of negotiation. The precondition is related not only to negotiating an overall settlement, but to a partial Suez Canal agreement. Egypt wishes to end the negotiations even before they begin. Thus, the rigidity of this position precludes progress toward peace.

Finally, there is the issue of the Arab refugees. I do not propose to reargue in detail the origins of this problem. That the exodus was instigated by the Arab leadership is readily demonstrated through Arab sources. To cite just one: "The Arab governments told us, "Go out so that we can get in.' So we got out, but they did not get in."[3] That the numbers of the authentic refugees have been grossly inflated through duplicate registrations and the accretion of Arabs from Syria, Jordan and Lebanon to the relief rolls has been revealed by every check of the UNRWA records. Nor do I seek to minimize the wretchedness and abnormality of unproductive existence in the camps. But who bears the responsibility for this situation?

The deliberate exploitation of the refugees for political ends began in 1948 and continues unabated to this day. The Arab governments have repeatedly rejected numerous lavish proposals for the solution

---

[3] Statement of an Arab refugee, quoted in *Al-Difaa* (Amman), September 6, 1954.

of the Arab refugee problem. They make no secret of their motivation. One quotation will suffice: "Any discussion aimed at a solution of the Palestine problem which will not be based on ensuring the refugees' right to annihilate Israel will be regarded as a desecration of the Arab people and an act of treason."[4] A policy of calculated incitement in the camps, whose dissolution the Arab leadership refuse to permit, has kept the pot boiling. As the role of second-generation refugees begins to wear thin, there has appeared the image of the Palestinian terrorist sworn to "dismantle" Israel.

Israel has an indigenous minority of nearly half a million Arabs, constituting approximately 15 percent of the population. Israeli Arabs are equal citizens whose welfare and integration are our natural concern. But we cannot accept the repatriation of those who originally joined our enemies and in the intervening years have become a hostile army proposing to submerge Israel. And obviously we have no common language with Palestinian irredentists, whose cry is the "liquidation" of Israel, or assassins who pretend to the name of "revolutionaries."

During the few years since the Six Day War, the position of the refugees in the areas administered by Israel has undergone substantial improvement — in employment, in education, in health and in living standards. This human progress indicates what might have been achieved during the 20 years prior to 1967 had Arab governments behaved humanely toward the refugees — their own kith and kin — rather than exploit them as a political weapon against Israel.

So long as the ceasefire remains intact, we shall continue to do all we can to relieve the refugees of the misery of the camps and restore to them their human dignity. A complete solution of the refugee problem, however, will come about only when the Arab states assume their full responsibility within the vast geography that is at their disposal.

Is the conflict then irreconcilable? Let me answer plainly: I do not consider Israel's right to existence a theme for discussion. As long as all Arab designs are predicated on the immediate or eventual destruction of Israel, no progress toward peace is possible. At the same time, we believe that the differences between us and the Arabs are soluble, and that because of the genuine needs of the peoples of the Middle East reason will finally prevail. International funds, toward which Israel is prepared to contribute her share (we have offered

---

[4]Resolution adopted at Refugee Conference, Syria, July 1957.

compensation for Arab property in Israel), are available for the resettlement of Arab refugees still living in camps. Between the Mediterranean and Iraq — the original area of Mandatory Palestine — there is room for both a Jewish and an Arab state. The name of the Arab state and its internal constitution and order are its responsibility and concern.

I still hope that, in a world that has just seen the close of the Vietnamese conflict through negotiation and a movement toward coexistence among the great powers, the many sovereign Arab states will come to terms with the idea of Jewish national independence and with the reality of Israel, the one small land in which that independence can flourish. Genuine peace requires more than a signature to an agreement. That signature is a beginning; it is the passage to a bridge of understanding and of cooperation between nations across which will move people, ideas and goods. My vision of peace is regional exchange and cooperation. And who can deny that there is much to be done for the good of this area? We do not make this a condition for signing a peace agreement. We register it as an expression of the quality of relations we would wish to see develop between ourselves and our neighbors in peace.

What is Zionism?

Zionism is the modern expression of the ancient Jewish heritage.

Zionism is the national liberation movement of a people exiled from its historic homeland and dispersed among the nations of the world.

Zionism is the redemption of an ancient nation from a tragic lot and the redemption of a land neglected for centuries.

Zionism is the revival of an ancient language and culture, in which the vision of universal peace has been a central theme.

Zionism is the embodiment of a unique pioneering spirit, of the dignity of labour, and of enduring human values.

Zionism is creating a society, however imperfect it may still be, which tries to implement the highest ideals of democracy — political social and cultural — for all the inhabitants of Israel, irrespective of religious belief, race or sex.

Zionism is, in sum, the constant and unrelenting effort to realize the national and universal vision of the prophets of Israel.

Yigal Allon at U.N. General Assembly, September 30, 1975.

The Jews and Jerusalem

In the course of its history, Jerusalem has known many rulers. But only for the Jews, three times in its history, has it been the capital of the nation living in this Land. From 1000 BCE, it was the capital of the Kingdom of David and his successors. From 516 BCE until the destruction of the Second Temple in 70 CE, it was again the capital of the Jewish people. In 1948, it became our capital once more.

At all other times Jerusalem was ruled by foreigners, who treated it as a provincial town: Babylonians in the sixth century BCE; Greeks in the second century BCE; Romans in the years 70-324 CE; Byzantines in 324-614 and the Persians briefly after them; Arabs in 638-1099; Crusaders in 1099-1187; Ayyubids and Mamluks in 1187-1517; Ottomans in 1517-1917; British from 1917 to 1948. Between 1948 and 1967, a part of the city was ruled by Jordan from the Hashemite capital in Amman.

The Jews of Jerusalem today are the inhabitants with the longest unbroken historical association with it. Their memory of it is recorded in the Bible, the Mishna and the Talmud, in prayer and poetry. Three times a day, for nineteen hundred years, Jews have prayed to return to Jerusalem. Once every year, on Tisha b'Av (the ninth day of the month of Av), they have fasted and mourned the destruction of Jerusalem. On festivals, they bless each other: 'Next year in Jerusalem!'

This bond of Jewish memory is engraved upon the ancient stones of Jerusalem and structures now being uncovered by archaeologists. Remnants have been revealed of the City of David and the days of the First Temple, and of the period of the Second Temple. The

Western Wall of the Second Temple still stands, a focus of Jewish longing for nineteen centuries.

The story of Jewish attachment to Jerusalem under alien dominion is an unremitting struggle to preserve a Jewish presence in it, never allowing the link to be broken. The Babylonians destroyed the city — seventy years later the Jews were rebuilding it. The Romans destroyed it and changed its name to Aelia Capitolina, and the Bar-Kokhba revolt of 132-135 CE, which cost half a million Jewish lives, was a last desperate attempt to oust the Romans and free Jerusalem. The Byzantines denied Jews the right to live in Jerusalem. The Crusaders massacred the Jewish population of the city. The Jordanian Government destroyed the ancient Jewish Quarter in the Old City and barred Jews from entry, even as tourists.

Yet despite bans and persecutions, Jews maintained an almost continuous presence in Jerusalem. When expelled, they always returned. From time to time, they were even helped by foreign rulers:

• In 515 BCE, Cyrus of Persia allowed the Jews to return to Jerusalem from exile in Babylon, re-build the city and revive their national life.

• In 362 CE, the Roman emperor Julian 'the Apostate' promised the Jews that he would restore Jerusalem to them and sanction the reconstruction of the Temple.

• The Persians who took Jerusalem in 614 CE handed it over to the Jews, and for the next three years it was ruled by Jews.

• The Caliph Abd el-Malik, who built the Dome of the Rock in 691 CE, gave Jewish families hereditary rights as caretakers on the Temple Mount.

Jerusalem Under Foreign Rule

More often than not under foreign rule Jerusalem fell into decay. When Jews were allowed to re-enter, it prospered again. Before the destruction of the Second Temple, Jerusalem had a population of 200,000; subsequently it became a provincial townlet. Under the Byzantines, the population was 80,000. After the Arab conquest in the seventh century, it declined to 30,000. In early Crusader times, it was as low as 3,000. Then it rose to 30,000, only to drop back to 10,000 towards the end of the Mamluk period. Under the Ottomans, it ranged between 10,000 and 15,000.

The Jews were the first, in the mid-19th century, to build new quarters outside the Wall of the Old City. From then on, there was a rapid rise in the city's population, and in the proportion of Jews in it. It is now more than a hundred years since the Jews again became, and remained, a majority.

Although the Jews have been a majority of the population for over a century, under British rule (1918-1948) Jerusalem was administered throughout by a municipality with an Arab or British mayor. Only after the establishment of Israel could the inhabitants of the Jewish part elect a municipality of their own. But, for nineteen years, it was a city divided.

Jerusalem — Capital of Israel

In 1948, Jerusalem became once more the capital of a sovereign Jewish State. Jerusalem is the seat of the President, of the Knesset (parliament), the Supreme Court, the Government Ministries, the Chief Rabbinate, the Jewish Agency, the headquarters of the Zionist Movement, and many major religious and cultural Jewish institutions.

In 1967, Jerusalem became once more a single, unified city, and nineteen years of abnormal division, of barbed wire and concrete barriers, came to an end. Never before in its history had Jerusalem been thus divided. Reunified, it remains the capital of Israel, spiritual shrine and centre of all Jews on earth. In reunified Jerusalem, the Jews remain the majority that they had been for the past hundred and more years.

Jerusalem And Christianity

The Christian link with Jerusalem begins with Jesus of Nazareth and the traditional association of many places in the city with the story of his life and death. This is essentially a religious link with no element of national culture in it. It is neither political nor secular. In the course of time, many places of worship were built by Christians of various denominations, such as the Orthodox (Greek, Syrian and Armenian), Catholics (Greek and Roman), Copts, Ethiopians, Protestants and Anglicans. But for no Church, then or now, does Jerusalem represent its world centre. Churches with a world centre have established it anywhere but in Jerusalem; for instance, the Catholic Church in Rome.

Three times in its history Jerusalem was ruled by Christians: in the Byzantine period, as a provincial town in which Christian institutions predominated; under Crusader rule when conquerors from Western Europe repressed the rights of Moslems and Jews and kept them out of the city; under the British Mandate, officials of a foreign empire were in control. Politics impelled Britain from time to time to contrive a strange 'balancer' between denominational claims and needs. For example, the appointment of an Arab mayor, although the majority of the population was Jewish, and the restriction of religious practice for the Jews at their holiest shrine, the Western Wall, where they were forbidden to blow the ram's horn on Rosh Hashanah and the Day of Atonement.

The British did not suceed in keeping the city quiet or in preventing outbreaks of Arab violence against the Jews in 1920 and 1929, in 1936-39, and in 1947-48. Unrest and inter-communal tension at times disrupted access to the Holy Places. It is possible that this unrest and its consequences suited the interests of the Mandatory Power.

Christian Churches in Jerusalem — The 'Status Quo'

Churches of diverse denominations are active in Jerusalem. Their rights in the places holy to Christianity were defined in the course of the 19th century, under what has been known since Ottoman days as the *status quo*. It remained in force throughout the period of the British Mandate and is in force in Israel today.

The *status quo* is based on a distinction between religious rights and secular authority. It is not contingent on the city being administered by the followers of any particular religion. It does not depend on Christians sharing in the secular authority as an expression and assertion of their due rights in the places holy to them. Nor have Christians ever claimed by law or theology that those places should be under Arab political sovereignty and no other.

Christian Population In Jeruslaem

The Christian population of Jerusalem was 3,390 in 1844; it rose gradually to 31,300 in 1946. From then on, it dwindled. Many Arab Christians, as well as non-Arab Christians — for example, British civil servants — left Jerusalem as the violence erupted which culminated in the 1948 war. After that, the hostility of the Jordanian Government led more Christians to leave. In 1961, the Christian population was 10,980. After the Six-Day War, the figure was 10,800. In 1970, it was 11,300. The continued trickle of emigration is more than compensated by the rate of natural increase. The rate of emigration has slowed down substantially since 1967: between 1967 and 1970, an average of some 130 Christian Arabs left each year, against an annual average of over 1,000 in the first twelve years of Jordanian rule.

Jerusalem And Islam

Jerusalem's first encounter with Islam, in the seventh century, was also its first encounter with the Arabs who were Islam's apostles and, under its banner, acquired a vast empire from the Persian Gulf to the Atlantic Ocean. Moslem Arabs ruled Jerusalem till the end of the eleventh century, that is, for about 480 years. Arab rule was not renewed until 1948 when, under the command of British officers, Trans-Jordanian troops seized part of the eastern city and proceeded to administer it for nineteen years. (There were Moslem rulers in Jerusalem at other times, but they were generally Kurds, Turks and others, not Arabs.)

To understand the place of Jerusalem in Islam, we must go back to the time of the Prophet Mohammed. In the first years of his ministry among the Arab tribes, he set out to befriend the Jews of the Arabian Peninsula. To win them over, he ordained that every believer face Jerusalem in his prayers, as was the custom of the Jews. But this brought no Jewish converts, and, in 623, he bade the faithful turn to Mecca. In the Sura 'The Cow' of the Koran we read:

'We appointed the "Qiblah" (direction) towards which thou didst formerly pray only that we might know him who followeth the messenger of God from him who turneth back on his heels.'

Pilgrimage to Mecca was prescribed by Mohammed as a first and fundamental duty of believers. Visiting Jerusalem is regarded not as a true pilgrimage *(hajj),* but a brief sojourn *(ziara):* pilgrims would call in at Jerusalem on their way back from Mecca, and the faithful sometimes felt that the sight of Jerusalem made up a little for failure to perform the *hajj* itself.

At the outset of Arabian rule, the Dome of the Rock was built as a monument on the Temple Mount (691) over the spot where — according to tradition — the Patriarch Abraham bound his son for the sacrifice and the Temple had later stood. Subsequently the El-Aqsa mosque (El-Aqsa means 'the edge') was built in a corner of the Mount. In the course of time, it became the third mosque in Moslem sanctity after the shrines of Mecca and Medina, being connected with the tradition that, from nearby, Mohammed rose to heaven.

That Moslem theology does not require that there be Moslem political sovereignty over Jerusalem is proved by the acceptance of internationalization by Arab States. At no moment of Moslem rule, whether by Arabs or non-Arabs, was Jerusalem a political capital. It was never the capital of a State, or even of a province. The Omayyad Caliph Suleiman (715-717 CE) commanded that Damascus remain the capital of his kingdom and Ramla was built as the administrative centre of the district to which Jerusalem belonged. It never occurred to him — or to any of his successors — to make Jerusalem their capital.

The Arabs And Jerusalem

Arab control of Jerusalem began in 638 CE: in that year the soldiers of Caliph Omar occupied the city after a long siege. The conquerors allowed the Jewish and Christian inhabitants to stay. This was an act of tolerance, but its implementation reflected the tenet of Islam that Jews and Christians were persons of inferior status. That status was expressed in the enforcement of a poll-tax upon them, in the wearing of garments that would identify them on sight and in other ways.

Aràb rule in Jerusalem was marked by insecurity and ferment. First, the Omayyad Caliphs ruled from Damascus, then the Abbasids from Baghdad in 750 CE, then in 969 CE the Fatimids from Cairo. In Omayyad days, Jerusalem was of little account. The founding of Ramla in the eighth century as provincial centre and the transfer of the imperial capital from Damascus to Baghdad left Jerusalem even further away from the centres of power and cultural activity.

The period was marked by occasional destruction or confiscation of Christian churches and Jewish synagogues and a sporadic persecution of their worshippers. In 966 CE, a mob inflamed by agents of the Caliphate set fire to the Church of the Holy Sepulchre and the Church on Mount Zion, and murdered Patriarch John. Confiscated churches were made into mosques. Bigotry and oppression persisted through the reign of Caliph el-Hakim (1009-1020 CE); the rebuilt Church of the Holy Sepulchre was destroyed and many other churches and synagogues were destroyed with it.

Arab rule returned to Jerusalem in 1948 when a Trans-Jordanian army, led by a British officer, overran the eastern part of the city. This was after the Arab States had rejected the decision of the General Assembly of the United Nations in 1947 to partition Mandatory Palestine into a Jewish and an Arab State and to internationalize Jerusalem.

After the war of 1948, all the Arab States, except Trans-Jordan, altered their stand and championed internationalization, with the aim of keeping Israel out. In April 1950, Jordan (having changed its name for the occasion) annexed the areas which it had occupied, including East Jerusalem.

The other Arab States then convened the Arab League with the intention of expelling Jordan from these areas, but a compromise was reached: the Arab States agreed to view the annexed areas as held in 'chancery' by Jordan, while Jordan viewed them as permanent parts of the Hashemite Kingdom. Jordan's occupation of East Jerusalem ended in June 1967, after it had deliberately opened war in the city.

In August 1969, the El-Aqsa mosque was set on fire by a deranged Christian tourist, whereupon Arab spokesmen charged Israel with arson. Israel, in fact, helped to prevent the mosque from being burnt to the ground by instantly summoning fire brigades to the scene; firemen from towns in the West Bank and in Israel subdued the flames. For political reasons, the Moslem Waqf Administration, which is responsible for the management and upkeep of the mosque, tried to prevent repairs. The repairs were eventually begun against the wishes of Jordan, but with Egyptian backing.

Jerusalem Population: Development From 1844 To 1973

Year	Jews	Moslems	Christians	Total
1844	7,120	5,000	3,390	15,510
1876	12,000	7,560	5,470	25,030
1896	28,112	8,560	8,748	45,420
1905	40,000	7,000	13,000	60,000
1910	47,000	9,800	16,400	73,600
1922	33,971	13,413	14,699	62,578
1931	51,222	19,894	19,335	90,451
1948	100,000	40,000	25,000	165,000
1967*	195,700	54,963	10,800**	261,463
1970**	215,500	61,600	11,500	288,600
1973*	222,100	67,000	12,000	301,100

*The figures refer to the area of Greater Jerusalem
**In 1961 the number of Christians in Jerusalem under Jordanian rule was 10,980.

The Question of Boundaries

How valid is the Arab claim to the occupied territories?

The boundaries of Near East countries were fixed largely by the Great Powers after the defeat of the Ottoman Empire in World War I. None of the current borders are sanctified by more than 70 years of history; lines were drawn arbitrarily and with little regard for economic or strategic necessity.

Under the Romans, Palestina was divided into three interdependent districts: Judea and Samaria; the Galilee and Transjordan; and the Negev. The Moslem caliphates combined the three districts into two: Falastin and Al Urdan (Jordan). The Arabs adopted the geographic definition "Palestine," which the Romans had created to erase even the memory of Jewish sovereignty.

The Ottoman Empire redrew the map. The Vilayet of Sidon ran along the Mediterranean coast, from Latakia south to Jaffa. The Vilayet of Damascus ran south and included Transjordan and the center of Palestine down to Nablus.

The Vilayet of Aleppo was to the north of these two regions.

The remainder of what was later to be known as Palestine, from Jaffa to the Sinai Peninsula and eastward to the Jordan River, was a separate district called the Sanjak of Jerusalem.

"Egypt Always Owned The Sinai."

Many boundary lines in Asia and Africa have been fixed by Great Powers in the service of their own interests. Thus ironically Egypt

From Near East Report, *1974.*

owes her ownership of the Sinai peninsula to the British.

And it is an ironic sequel that today Egypt wants the Great Powers to help her regain the Sinai, which she lost to Israel in the Six-Day War in 1967.

The Sinai peninsula has been one of the most crossed, but least occupied, pieces of real estate on the earth.

At the beginning of the modern era, in 1517, the Turkish Sultan, Selim I, took the Sinai route to conquer Egypt, beginning more than 400 years of Turkish suzerainty. During this period an Egyptian Pasha appointed by the Sultan ruled Egypt and bits and pieces of Sinai, then known as Arabia Petraea. Napolean threatened Turkish domination when he subdued Egypt and used the Sinai as a convenient highway to conquer the Levant. But the Turkish Janissary drove the French out of the desert — and all of Egypt — in 1800.

So it remained until the restless Pasha of Egypt, Mohammed Ali, under the generalship of his son, Ibrahim, crossed the Sinai in 1831. Encouraged by victories in Palestine, Syria and Anatolia, he threatened Constantinople itself by the end of the decade.

However, European powers, under the leadership of Great Britain, saved the Turks and forced Ibrahim back to the Nile, where the Sultan told Ali: "I grant unto thee the Government of Egypt within its ancient boundaries. . . ."

However, the Sultan permitted Egypt to administer the northwestern wedge of Sinai — not because it was within Egypt's "ancient boundaries" or because of previous territorial claims, but in order to compensate Ali for relinquishing his administration of Crete. The proclamation established the Rafa to Suez border lines — the first defined frontiers between Egyptain-administered Sinai and Turkish Sinai.

Completion of the Suez Canal in 1869 enhanced importance of the Sinai peninsula as a buffer to protect the east bank of the Canal, and the British, who had entered Egypt in force in 1882, maneuvered to enlarged it.

The distrustful Turks tried to weaken and erode the Sinai buffer. But British *de facto* control of Egyptain affairs became irresistible and a new arrangement was forced on the Sublime Porte.

In 1892 a new frontier was drawn from the vicinity of Rafa to the head of the Gulf of Aqaba. And only then did the present Sinai frontier take shape.

In 1905-6 Abdul Hamid, the Turkish Sultan, made a determined attempt to regain the Sinai. But he failed, and the 1892 arrangements were confirmed.

This line was not a border in its classical sense. Egypt was still part of the Ottoman Empire. The Rafa-Aqaba line merely separated the Ottoman area from the Anglo-Egyptian administered area. As Egyptian affairs were entirely decided by the imperial interests of Great Britain, Egypt had little say in all these border disputes. Thus, Egyptian jurisdiction over the Sinai today is a direct result of British colonial policy.

When World War I threatened in 1914, the British moved to strengthen the Sinai buffer between the hostile Turks and the Suez Canal. They announced that the "suzerainty of Turkey over Egypt was terminated" and that Egypt was their protectorate.

Sinai became a battlefield. The Turks sent patrols into Sinai and harassed the British administrative center at Nakhl. In early 1915 the Turks attacked the canal itself. They failed and the tide in the Sinai turned.

At first Arab forces offered some token aid to the British, but as Major C.S. Jarvis, Governor of Sinai from 1923 to 1936, wrote: "The Arabs suffered considerable loss (at Tur-1916) and this appeared to satisfy their martial ardor, as they took no further part in the war. . . ." The British carried on alone and took Rafa.

The Sinai episode of World War I was over. British arms had secured the Sinai and their claims to it were, therefore, supported by the right of conquest. There was even some discussion of annexing Sinai, but President Wilson rejected the idea.

At the Lausanne Peace Conference in 1923, Turkey gave up all non-Turkish territories lost in the war. It renounced "rights and titles over Egypt."

Thus, along with Egypt, Great Britain also "inherited" the Sinai peninsula.

Anglo-Egyptian relations steadily worsened after World War I despite termination of the Protectorate and the granting of independence in 1922. The English finally agreed in 1936 to end their military occupation except in the immediate vicinity of the canal.

The Egyptians then moved in, inheriting the British colonial border. But Egypt — now becoming expansionist — was unwilling to abide by this frontier.

Egypt invaded the new State of Israel in 1948, in defiance of the

UN Partition Resolution. Egypt lost, and, as Israel forces crossed Sinai, nearing the Suez Canal, the British prepared to come to Egypt's assistance. Rather than accept the humiliation of support from the hated British, the Egyptians agreed to enter into an armistice agreement with the victorious Israelis.

A substitute for real peace, the General Armistice Agreement of February 1949 provided that the demarcation lines were "not to be construed in any sense as a political or territorial boundary." *(Par 5, subparagraph 2)*

In addition, the only function of the armistice line was "to delineate the line beyond which the armed forces of the respectives parties shall not move. . . ."

But the Egyptians would not sign a peace treaty which would have clearly defined the border.

Lebanon And Syria

After World War I, France and Britain carved up the region. The French took over the area now known as Lebanon and Syria; the British received the remainder of the Fertile Crescent states: Palestine and Iraq.

In 1923, the League of Nations recognized the French mandates. Soon borders were again redrawn. In 1926 Lebanon was separated from Syria and was made an independent state. It was enlarged to include Beirut, Tripoli, Sidon, the Biqa Valley and the region to the Palestine border. This meant that Lebanon would have enough Christians to justify a separate government and enough Moslems to warrant the need for continued French protection. The waters of the Litani River were given to Lebanon at French insistence. The French had deposed Faisal in Syria.

To assuage him, Britain installed him as the ruler of the new kindom of Iraq. Later, in 1922 the British put Faisal's brother, Abdullah, on the throne of the newly-created Transjordan.

The boundaries of Palestine also reflected British-French agreement.

"The West Bank Belongs To Jordan."

The Jordan River was the frontier between Palestine and Transjordan after 1922.

Foreign Relations of the United States, 1947, The Near East, published a declassified dispatch of Nov. 21, 1947 from Nicholas Haiji Vasselou, then Greek charge d'affaires to Transjordan. Vasselou wrote: "King Abdullah did state that his army would occupy

Palestine land to the west and the north and that 6,000 desert legionnaires were already in Palestine. . . . It is obviously Abdullah's intention to keep as much as possible of those parts of Palestine allocated to the Arabs" by UNSCOP.

In 1948, Abdullah's Arab Legion invaded Palestine, seizing the West Bank and the Old City of Jerusalem. Transjordan formally annexed the West Bank in 1950, changing its name to Jordan.

Under the partition resolution, the West Bank had been allocated to the Palestine Arab state and West Bank Arabs opposed Jordan's takeover.

Only two governments, Britain and Pakistan, recognized the annexation *de jure.*

The United States never recognized Jordan's annexation *de jure.* Nor did the United States recognize Jordan's occupation of the Old City.

Golan Heights

This range was part of Syria. It was a strategic asset. Overlooking the northern part of Israel, it was used for 20 years as a base for attacks on Israel settlers and fishermen, and for plans to prevent Israel from drawing her share of the Jordan River sources.

Gaza

This strip along the Mediterranean Coast was allotted to the proposed Arab state under the partition resolution but was seized and held by Egyptain forces for 20 years, until the Six-Day War.

"Acquisition Of Territory By Force Is Inadmissable. The Arabs And The Soviets Insist Upon This."

Czarist Russia and the USSR both have been unparalleled land-grabbers. The tiny Principality of Moscow expanded a hundred-fold by armed conquest over five centuries. According to the Barnes and Noble *Historical Atlas of the World* (Maps 72 and 97), Russia absorbed, in chronological order, the Moscow hinterland, Novgorod, the Khanate of Khazan, the Khanate of Astrakhan, Polish Smolensk, Ingria, Estonia, Karelia, Livonia, the Khanate of the Crimea, the Ukraine, Lithuania, East Poland, Central Poland, Moldavia and the South Caucasus.

Russian acquisitions in the 19th century alone: West Turkestan, Bokhara, Turkmenistan, Southwest Caucasus, Amur province and Sakhalin. A few of these areas (the Baltic states and East Europe) were deeded to other states or granted independence.

All these Czarist acquisitions by force inspired the Soviet imperialists who carved up Europe after World War II. The Soviet Union seized or reabsorbed: Karelia (from Finland); Latvia, Lithuania and Estonia (all previously independent); Galicia and East Poland (from Poland); Bessarabia (from Germany); the Kurile islands (from Japan).

In addition, the USSR redrew the map: South Dobruja and South Moldavia were taken from Rumania and given to Bulgaria; West Prussia, and part of East Prussia, the heart of Germany, were attached to Poland.

Unimpressed by international niceties, the USSR kicked out Germans, Poles and Finns where their presence conflicted with the new nationality of the land. No one mentioned compensation or resettlement, let alone repatriation to "stolen lands."

In 1948, Egypt absorbed Sinai and Gaza; Jordan took over the West Bank; the Saudis conquered their domain from competing local sheikhs. Only with an Israel administration has an outcry arisen over the "inadmissability of territorial acquisition by force."

Zionism Today — The "Jerusalem Program"

The aims of Zionism are:

The unity of the Jewish people and the centrality of Israel in Jewish life;

The ingathering of the Jewish people in its historic homeland Eretz Yisrael through Aliyah from all countries;

The strengthening of the State of Israel, founded on the Prophetic ideals of justice and peace;

The preservation of the identity of the Jewish people through the fostering of Jewish and Hebrew education and of Jewish spiritual and cultural values;

The protection of Jewish rights everywhere.

(Adopted by the 27th World Zionist Congress, Jerusalem, June 1968)

PALESTINE ~ THE JEWISH NATIONAL HOME, 1919

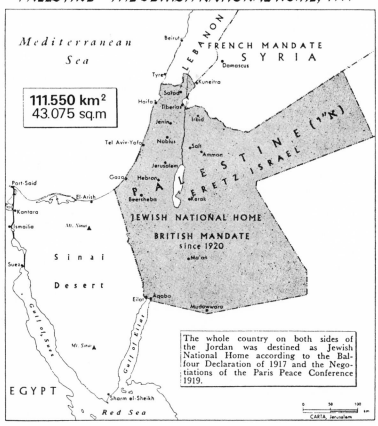

The whole country on both sides of the Jordan was destined as Jewish National Home according to the Balfour Declaration of 1917 and the Negotiations of the Paris Peace Conference 1919.

THE JEWISH NATIONAL HOME
AFTER THE FIRST PARTITION OF PALESTINE, 1922

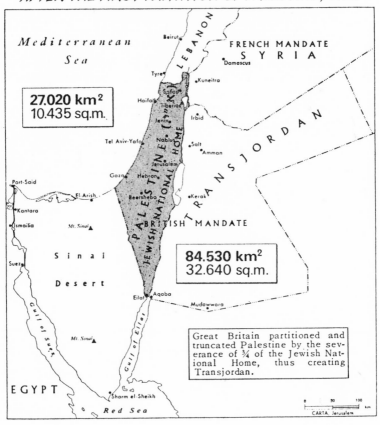

ISRAEL-ARMISTICE LINES 1949-1967

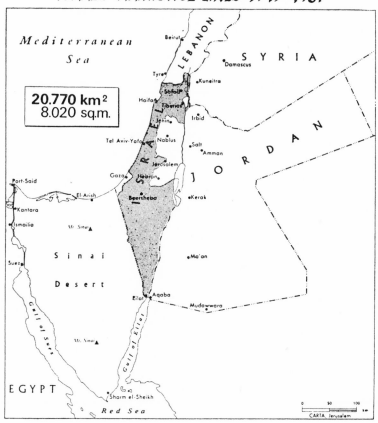

ISRAEL CEASE-FIRE LINES SINCE 1967